VOLUME 91 • NUMBER 1 • SPRING 2002

NATIONAL

CIVIC

REVIEW

MAKING CITIZEN DEMOCRACY WORK

IN THIS ISSUE

Issues in Local Government Structure and Performance

Christopher T. Gates

President, National Civic League

Robert Loper

Editor

A Publication of the National Civic League and Jossey-Bass

NATIONAL CIVIC REVIEW (ISSN 0027-9013) is published quarterly by Wiley Subscription Services, Inc., a Wiley company, at Jossey-Bass, 989 Market Street, San Francisco, CA 94103-1741, and the National Civic League, 1445 Market Street, Suite 300, Denver, CO 80202-1717. NCL, founded in 1894 as the National Municipal League, advocates a new civic agenda to create communities that work for everyone. NCL is a 501(c)(3) nonprofit, non-partisan educational association of individuals and organizations. NCL members have access to the information and services necessary to improve community life. For complete information, contact Derek Okubo, (303) 571-4343.

INDEXED in Public Affairs Information Service, ABC POL SCI, and Book Review Index.

SUBSCRIPTIONS are $55.00 per year for individuals and $105.00 per year for institutions. To order subscriptions, single issues, or reprints, please refer to the Ordering Information page at the back of this issue.

PERIODICALS postage paid at San Francisco, California, and at additional mailing offices. POSTMASTER: send address changes to *National Civic Review,* Jossey-Bass Inc., 989 Market Street, San Francisco, CA 94103-1741.

NCL MEMBERS send change of address to Debbie Gettings, National Civic League, 1445 Market Street, Suite 300, Denver, CO 80202-1717.

EDITORIAL CORRESPONDENCE should be sent to Robert Loper, National Civic League, 1319 F Street NW, Suite 204, Washington, DC 20004.

www.josseybass.com

LETTERS TO THE EDITOR. *National Civic Review* welcomes letters to the editor. Write to *National Civic Review,* 1319 F Street, Suite 204, Washington, DC 20004, or send e-mail to robert@ncldc.org. Please include your name, address, and telephone number.

CONTENTS

Ted Halstead, Michael Lind

The technological changes being ushered in by the Information Age will have lasting effects on the public, private, and nonprofit sectors of American society. In this article, the authors consider the prospective impact of these developments on civil society and highlight challenges dealing with race, intergenerational differences, and the possibilities presented by genetic engineering.

NOTE FROM THE PRESIDENT

From its inception, the National Civic League has focused on the importance of municipal government reform to the quality of our political life. Long-time readers of this journal will need no review of NCL's role in developing and updating model city charters. As the charter revision project (http://nclweb.org/npp/charter/process.html) moves forward, we are again devoting an edition of the *National Civic Review* to issues of local government structure and performance. The articles collected here examine everything from charters themselves to the role and position of the mayor, the city council, and the chief administrative officer in various forms of local government.

As the presentations at last year's National Conference on Governance made clear, information technology is having a profound effect on the practice of politics in this country. At every stage of the process, from raising money and disseminating information to enhancing transparency, improving service delivery, and encouraging participation, this technology is not only accelerating the pace of political activity but perhaps even changing its nature. Taken together, these multifaceted changes are a particularly telling example of how politics and political actors influence and are influenced by ongoing developments in society as a whole.

The flip side of this engagement in the swirl of events is government structure, which is why constructs such as a municipal charter are so important. By establishing roles and responsibilities, a charter helps ensure stability in the governance of a community. Without trying to sketch a theory of politics here, it is useful to think of political practices (such as voting and law-making) as being embedded in networks—institutions and institutional relations—that are in turn governed by norms and values. Municipal charters are part of the codification of institutional relations and lend order and stability to the political system.

That said, a charter itself must be adapted to changing circumstances, which is why the model city charter is again being revised. There is a litany (by now familiar) of problems and pressures with which communities continue to grapple. Issues of economic development, land use, sprawl, housing, schools, health care, and crime are but some of the most obvious. Except for a narrow class of essentially technical questions (which, despite this status, have significant real-world implications), a charter by itself cannot solve these political problems. A poorly designed charter can make political issues more intractable; a well-designed charter can mitigate certain problems while enhancing the prospects for progress in others. But most of all, just as a government budget is a political document that indicates policy priorities, a charter is a blueprint for the kind of political practice a city regards as desirable.

At the local level, the political arena is being reshaped by numerous developments, not the least of which is the increasing use of information technology. These changes are shifting existing patterns of authority and divisions of responsibility among the principal officials in both council-manager and mayor-council forms of government. In a number of cities, council members are playing a more activist role vis-à-vis the city manager, and mayors are consolidating their authority. At the same time, new avenues are opening for citizen participation in governance processes. In response to these developments, an increasing number of cities are deliberating over whether and how to make basic changes in their governance structures.

To help make the process of deliberation clear, the articles printed here offer insightful analysis of styles of mayoral leadership, the changing role of the city council, and the characteristics of the chief administrative officer. A number of the articles are closely integrated with each other. James H. Svara introduces a framework for assessing the city council by the type of role it performs and analyzes the trend toward greater council activism. Craig M. Wheeland's piece refines earlier work by Svara in distinguishing among mayoral types and qualities of mayoral leadership. Wheeland developed his set of types using the forty most populous cities in the United States. In her work, Kimberly L. Nelson identifies the characteristics of the chief administrative officers in the twenty-six most populous cities having a mayor-council form of government and examines the roles they play. Finally, Lawrence F. Keller gives a historical view of municipal charters and underscores their continuing importance to public life.

This issue is rounded out by complementary work that looks at the emergence of regional governance in the metropolitan Chicago area and by articles that examine the state of the civic renewal movement as well as look ahead to some of the divisions that may affect civil society in the years to come. The importance of devising regional solutions for regional problems has been evident for some time, but developing effective means for doing so has notably lagged this realization. In addition to the advances noted by David K. Hamilton in his article, there are some other promising efforts under way. The salience of regional governance and cross-sectoral collaboration continues to increase, and the *National Civic Review* will be part of the ongoing dialogue in this area.

The growth of the civic renewal movement also offers encouraging signs for the development of more comprehensive and citizen-based governance processes. Carmen Sirianni and Lewis A. Friedland review progress to date and issue a call for a "national civic congress" to reinforce these efforts and to ensure the movement's continuing momentum.

In their article, Ted Halstead and Michael Lind remind us of some of the challenges civil society faces in this century, ranging from persistent racial problems to exacerbation of generational tensions and the possible emergence of genetically engineered divisions.

A century ago, this country experienced a wave of progressive energy that led to substantive reform in government and governance. As the National Civic League again revises its model city charter, there are indications that another progressive wave is building.

CHRISTOPHER T. GATES
PRESIDENT, NATIONAL CIVIC LEAGUE

The Roles of the City Council and Implications for the Structure of City Government

James H. Svara

When exploring ways to improve the performance of city government, it is appropriate to devote considerable attention to the effects of structure on outcomes. It is also important to examine variations of behavior within as well as between structures of city government. The council-manager form of government, as outlined in the Model City Charter, assigns governmental authority to the council and allows the council to appoint and remove the city manager. Effective functioning of this form of government depends on the distinctive relationship between the council and the city manager and the ability of the council to play certain roles that contribute to sound governance.

The reform perspective argues that the council should determine the purpose and goals of city government and ensure that administrative performance accomplishes these goals. In a Goldilocks kind of situation, the council must provide not too much leadership or too little leadership, but just the right amount and the right kinds of leadership. The effectiveness of this form of government depends on council members' meeting these expectations. However, it has been difficult to specify exactly what the appropriate role for the council is, and expectations may be shifting. To understand council-manager government and how it differs from the mayor-council form, it is useful to explore the alternative roles that the council can play and seek to determine the impact of each role on the effectiveness of this form of government.

Changing conditions in American cities and changing characteristics of council members make it important to reexamine the role of the city council for two reasons. First, a clear understanding of baseline conditions is helpful in assessing the nature and impact of change. Second, changing conditions may alter the expectations we have of how the council should perform. What was ideal in the past may no longer be best suited for the present, or the future. Changing characteristics and behavior of city council members are producing a rethinking of the role of the council and how the mayor's position is defined, yielding some uncertainty about the viability of this form of government.

Although the primary focus of this discussion is the council-manager form, examining council roles under changing conditions also sheds light on the role of the elected official in a mayor-council government.

There are a variety of roles the council might fill—some positive and some negative, depending on one's point of view. Drawing on studies and observations of local government, one can identify five models on the basis of the kind of role the council could play in any local government. Each model is based on a central characteristic that defines the orientation of the council to policy making, representing citizens, and involvement in administrative matters. Of course, any actual city council evinces some mix of these characteristics. There are five models:

• In the *board of trustees* model, which is based on strict separation of politics and administration, the city council ultimately decides policy but is detached from the administrative activities of government and aloof from citizens. This model is often viewed as the ideal role for the council in the council-manager form, although I dispute this notion.

• In the *board of directors* model, the city council actively directs all aspects of city government, turning the city manager into their assistant. Although a division of function between policy and administration might be supported in theory, it is hard to place limits on the range of the council's involvement in administrative affairs.

• The *board of delegates* model—an alternative to the reform perspective—stresses the council member's acting as spokesperson for citizens in policy discussion and as ombudsman in addressing citizen complaints. This model implies that the executive is the primary source of policy innovation. The model may be common in the mayor-council form, where it is appropriate for the council to defer to the executive mayor since he or she is an elected official.

• The *board of governors* model is based on a pattern of interaction in which the council shapes overall goals, reviews and adopts proposals from the manager, and oversees the performance of administration. It has been the typical model in council-manager cities and, I argue, the traditional ideal model.

• The *board of activists* model appears to be an emerging model in which the board member is a policy activist and ombudsman for constituents. Given the orientation of the council and a short-term time perspective, the manager is not only an adviser and policy formulator but also an initiator of policy goals and projects.

In this article, each model is briefly explained and then the implications for council-manager relations (or council-mayor relations) are examined. Examining the five models helps to clarify trends in council-manager government and to highlight the differences between council-manager and mayor-council forms of government.

Board of Trustees: Too Little Leadership?

A simplistic starting point in discussing council-manager relations has been the dichotomy model, with strictly separated political and administrative spheres. The council role that corresponds to this view involves setting policy for city government. These decisions offer instructions to the city manager about the work that is to be done. As an approach to the way council members represent citizens, the trustee role implies that council members use their own judgment about what is best for the city rather than considering themselves to be instructed by or delegates of citizens. The council member is not directly involved in assisting citizens with complaints they have about city government. The city manager is an adviser to the council and implementer of their decisions.

The empirical shortcomings of a framework based on the dichotomy are extensive: local government does not (and never did) work this way in practice, and the relationship between elected officials and city managers is too close to support the idea that roles are strictly separated in local government. Although it has been common to presume that early municipal reformers and the creators of the second model city charter, which endorsed the council-manager form, were advocates of a dichotomy view, this is not the case. One selection from the commentary that accompanied the second model charter illustrates their thinking on relationships: "They are not two antagonistic elements, each seeking to enlarge its sphere of action at the expense of the other. They are not even independent powers in the government, each working in a distinct field, performing its appropriate acts, and having for these purposes an authority of its own. On the contrary, they are two parts of the same mechanism, or we may liken them to two elements in one chemical compound whose combined qualities give the character to the substance. In a sense, they take part jointly in every act performed."[1]

The early reformers wanted to keep partisan politics out of administration, and they did not want the city manager to be dictating policy; but they expected that the council would keep close track of administrative performance and that the manager would be a policy leader for the city. Although this model seems to put the manager in a subsidiary role to the council, the passivity and confined range of activities on the part of the council mean that the manager is the de facto major figure in city government. This approach is hard to justify as the preferred model of council behavior because the city manager can assume too large a role and the council can be reduced to a rubber-stamp position.

It is conceivable that the council could be a remote board that largely confines its activities to approving policy, but this approach is not common. This conclusion is based on analysis of a 1997 survey of city managers in the United States.[2] This survey indicated that in only 3 percent of the cities was it the case that city managers had substantial or high influence and the most important elected officials (the mayor, the council, or the committee chair) had low influence on decision making related to budget and economic development issues. The elected officials in those cities appear to be acting in ways described by the trustee model, accepting proposals largely shaped by the city manager. There is a risk in this situation that democratic forces may be secondary to professional perspectives and that the council is too aloof from the day-to-day functioning of city government and how it interacts with citizens.

Board of Directors: Too Much Leadership?

The title of this subsection is intended to convey the idea that in the board of directors model the members of the council are directly in charge of running city government and are involved in any aspect of city government in which they choose to intervene. Formally, all governmental authority resides in the city council, which sets the terms for how government operates. In contrast to the situation where the manager essentially creates the focus and direction of city government with a board of trustees council, a board of directors council is clearly in charge and the manager acts as their assistant. Exercising clear and continuous control, the directors may choose to closely supervise the manager and intervene in administrative matters directly or through orders to the manager. This model deviates from the ideal of the council-manager form by diminishing the contribution of the manager and potentially undermining his or her professionalism. It appears that this model is rarely found, although any council that seeks to dominate the manager and intervene in the operation of the city approximates it. It may be more common in small towns, particularly those with limited experience with council-manager government.

In the 1997 survey of city managers, characteristics approximating the board of directors model were found in only 1 percent of the cities. In these cities, elected officials exerted substantially greater influence than the city manager. Despite the possibility in the board of directors model that the council can overshadow the manager, the relationship between the council and the manager was generally positive.

Board of Delegates: Wrong Kind of Leadership?

In the board of delegates model, council members emphasize their linkage role to the citizen. They act as delegates with regard to policy matters—that is, the council members try to act as their constituents have instructed them to behave or, when questions arise, as their constituents would prefer. Since the council member's constituency is likely to be diverse, the member has an individual agenda and promotes his or her own separate point of view. Furthermore, the members act as an ombudsman assisting citizens with problems they have with city government. These matters range from helping constituents get information about a city program to intervening when the citizen has a complaint about treatment from staff or about delivery of a service. In this model, it is presumed that the executive is the driving force in promoting a policy program, and the council is placed in a more limited and reactive role. Given the centrality of the executive, it is important that this official be directly elected, to ensure direct citizen involvement in selecting the executive. This model therefore is appropriate for a mayor-council city rather than a council-manager city. It reflects emphasis on executive democracy rather than representative democracy, which is found in the council-manager city.

Board of Governors: Still-Just-Right Leadership?

The board of governors model exemplifies the main features of the council-manager form of government. Unlike the board of trustees or board of directors model, I would argue that this type is the "standard" or traditional model because it reflects the intentions of the early reformers who developed the second model charter. The characteristics of this model warrant elaboration in more detail.[3]

To understand the distinctive contributions of each set of officials in this model, it is useful to distinguish four dimensions of governmental decision making. Making decisions that determine goals and the "mission" of city government is the first dimension. Specifying the middle-range policies and programs that define goals is the second. Administration of policy is the third dimension; it involves implementation of programs and delivery of services to citizens. Finally, the fourth dimension is management of organizational resources in support of mission, policy, and administration.

In mission and policy, elected officials are goal setters who review and accept the recommendations of the city manager and policy enactors, and the city manager is an adviser regarding goals and a proposer of policy. Council members do more than merely accept or reject managerial proposals. The intimate relationship between the council and staff and the efforts of the manager to be attuned to the preferences of council members and to incorporate their ideas in his or her proposals means that council members have helped to shape the proposals they are considering. Council leadership makes an important difference when the council creates a clear framework of goals within which the city manager can operate.

In administration, elected officials are involved as overseers, and the city manager and staff are given freedom and flexibility to be implementers. In oversight, ideally the emphasis is placed on assessing how well programs are run and services are delivered and how well they meet their objectives. The council member is available to help constituents with service complaints but typically refers these matters to staff. With regard to the management dimension, the council role is limited but critically important. The elected official is an appointer of the city manager and appraiser of his or her performance. There is little involvement by the council in management activity.

The roles in the standard framework are overlapping and complementary.[4] Performance by one set of officials reinforces that of the other. Cooperative interaction between the two sets of officials is common. Filling a role in the way defined by this pattern produces governance on the basis of goals, long-term perspective, continuity, and linkage between intention and action in administrative systems. Stated differently, the city knows what it wants to do in the present and the future, stays on track, and organizes activities and allocates resources in terms of the goals it is trying to achieve. Accountability is high since the manager can be removed at any time, but it is general, with reliance on the systems created by the manager and staff for detailed control. The council may intervene in specific cases, but generally it relies on ultimate authority to hold the city manager accountable.

Thus, overall the manager proposes the course of action and the programs to meet goals set by the council and responds to council member preferences for policy, and the manager directs the administrative organization. The council members—like trustees in the sense that they are somewhat detached—dispose and review much more than they innovate or intervene, but the council can shape the goals and priorities of the city, ensure that the city is on track in achieving them, and through its hiring and review of the city manager make certain that high standards for organizational performance are maintained. Council members and city managers and staff have differing perspectives and bring different values and backgrounds to the governmental process. Still, when the council acts as a board of governors, the roles combine rather seamlessly with a high degree of coordination and little disagreement over who should do what. The council members are not simply reacting to a manager who exercises much more influence as the trustees do; there is deference on the part of the council to the manager and an apparent tendency to look to the manager for direction in determining how goals are met.

Estimating the proportion of cities that match the characteristics of the board of governors model is somewhat difficult. The overwhelming majority of city managers in the 1997 survey report that elected officials and the manager have a similar amount of influence, either equal or one slightly higher or lower than the other.[5] The cities in which the city manager has slightly greater influence—36 percent of the total—may approximate the board of governors model. The cities where elected officials had greater influence (18 percent) or equal influence (34 percent) may match the governor model or reflect a new role for the council: a board of activists.

Board of Activists: Too Much, Wrong Kind, or New-Just-Right?

Unlike the other models that have clear conceptual content, the description of the board of activists model is based on observation of behavior and surveys of attitudes of council members and managers. In this new formulation, it is not clear whether this is a coherent separate model or a blend of other models. Many people filling a council position today are electoral activists who deal with current problems, advocate policies, and help their constituents by being their spokesperson and representative. In this sense, they share some characteristics with the delegates. Data from surveys in large council-manager cities indicate that the council member is highly engaged in resolving citizen complaints and in dealing with pressing issues, and less involved in setting goals and strategies than twenty years ago.[6] In short, these elected officials are activists and problem solvers rather than broad policy makers, and they are regularly involved in ombudsman activities. They have more influence and impact on shaping policy than do delegates. In a council-manager city, the elected official has greater opportunity to intervene with the manager and other staff members regarding citizen complaints than in a mayor-council city because the institutional and political power of the mayor constrained the council in complaint handling. In this sense, an elected official in a council-manager city may display (or at least attempt to display) tendencies of a director.

The kinds of tasks pursued by the council member in this activist model work against development of cohesion among members and commitment to common goals because each council member has his or her own separate agenda. They do not present the broad view and focus on long-term goals as in the board of governors model, and they can even manifest the reactive qualities (but not the remoteness) characteristic of council members in the board of trustees model. In the absence of forces that promote cohesion on the council, the activist orientation can change the nature of interaction with the city manager. If the activist orientation becomes dominant on the council, it may be necessary to have a mayor who is effective at pulling council members together. If political leadership on the council is weak and council members emphasize current issues and are reluctant to make a long-term commitment, the city manager may need to become the originator of discussion about mission and goals. A pattern can emerge in which the manager stresses general policies that constitute a broad approach to governance, and the council focuses on alteration, adjustment, and exception responding to current circumstances and political pressure.

The behaviors observed in large cities—and confirmed anecdotally by managers in smaller cities—suggest new roles for council members in the activist model that differ from those found in the board of governors model. In the mission dimension, the council member is still a goal setter, but there is sometimes a question of whether the council member is legitimizing goals by giving them clear and long-term support or merely accepting them as "working" goals to be accepted tentatively. The level of commitment may be limited. The city manager is increasingly an initiator in mission as well as policy and actively promotes development of strategy and vision for the city. The manager encourages the council to consider mission decisions because the manager is aware of the need for and could be hampered by the absence of broad goals.

In policy, the council member is an advocate of policies and programs and wants to solve pressing problems. Although making policy decisions, the member gives more cautious and time-limited approval than in the past. The city manager is still the active policy initiator. At the same time, the manager is often put in the position of reacting to ideas being promoted by council members. On the occasion when the manager points out the possible negative implications of a proposal or raises questions about how it relates to other established goals and policies, the manager's response may appear negative to the council member making the proposal, and the manager may be viewed as an impediment to change. The manager also acts more as a broker or mediator helping to promote agreement and resolve conflict on the council.[7] Whereas in the past the manager would propose and the council dispose, now the manager is engaged in a broader range of activities trying to get agreement to his or her own proposals and to accommodate and deflect proposals from council members.

In administration, council members actively fill the ombudsman role. Increasingly they feel that their intervention is needed to ensure that citizen complaints are handled appropriately. Beyond handling complaints, they seek to guarantee that constituents receive the services they demand. In the past, when at-large elections were used more commonly, there was geographical, social, and racial distance between council members and segments of the population that had the greatest need for governmental services. It is probable that the council member to some extent moderated the requests that would come from citizens for expanded services. Now the member is more likely to be elected from a district and to enunciate service demands from constituents. Although still an overseer, the member spends less time on the evaluative aspect of this role than the members and administrators would prefer. The city manager continues as an implementer, but increasingly concerned with and being pushed by the council to be more attentive to responsiveness as well as the effectiveness of service delivery.

In management, the council member continues to appoint and appraise the city manager, but he or she is also actively interested in how management is carried out in the city. The member may push management initiatives such as privatization and contracting out. Drawing on higher involvement in citizen complaints, the council member has views about how staff are performing, and may be frustrated at not having a direct impact on staff appraisal, removal, and appointment. Although the council directly reviews only the manager, its interest in management extends beyond simply appraising the manager.

Thus the council members on a board of activists overlap more with the manager than do those on a board of governors. The boundary line between the spheres of each set of officials is more blurred, although distinctions remain. The city manager appears to devote more attention to discussing with council members where the boundary should be than in the past, when each was more comfortable with their respective role. Elected officials are more involved in administrative matters through complaint handling and are more interested in management. The city manager has always been involved in the highest level of policy making, but the involvement of managers in shaping the city's mission and goals is more visible because the manager is often pushing a council that is reluctant to take on these decisions. Increasingly, as one city manager remarked, council members feel that "mission is something managers do"—and something that council members do not. The complementary relationship that the city manager and activist elected officials have in this model features more give-and-take than is true in the board of governors model.

Differences Among Models

Table 1 presents a summary of the major characteristics of each model. There are clear shortcomings to the trustee, director, and delegate models. In a council-manager city, the trustees are remote and reactive and have a high level of dependence on a highly influential city manager. The directors are engaged but may not place limits on the extent of their involvement in the administrative and management dimensions and may ignore and undermine the professionalism and influence of the city manager. The delegates would not bring a broad view and independent judgment that the council should provide in a council-manager city, and in a mayor-council city their contribution is often limited to responding to proposals from the mayor in a way that reflects the preferences of their constituents. They are active, but the mayor's high influence, formal authority, and political resources may constrain the extent of the council's contributions and impact. The board of delegates council does, however, serve the crucial purpose of standing in for citizens in raising issues and solutions to problems and in reviewing and approving the proposals of the mayor.

The board of governors has been the ideal for council-manager cities and has in the past been commonly found. It is concerned with setting goals, determining how well policy advances goals, overseeing administration to "evaluate" how effectively and how well policies are being implemented, and appraising management to assess how well the organization is performing. The challenge for this council is to balance its emphasis on broad aspects of governance with attention to representation in order to achieve an appropriate level of political responsiveness—incorporating citizen views and addressing current concerns that may not be consistent with a long-term agenda—and administrative accountability by administrators. The board of governors model also implies an active city manager who interacts closely with the council in a manner characterized by mutual dependence and reciprocal influence. City managers clearly prefer that council members adopt roles that are derived from this model. There is a question, however, as to whether the board of governors council is viable unless it incorporates some of the elements of the board of

Table 1. Comparison of Five Models of Council Member Roles

Dimension	Board of Trustees	Board of Directors	Board of Governors	Board of Activists	Board of Delegates
Mission	Goal approver	Goal setter	Goal setter	Goal setter or ratifier	Goal approver
Policy	Ratifier; reacts to problems	Initiator; handles or delegates all problems	Enactor; focuses on long-term problems	Cautious enactor; seeks solutions to current problems; makes policy adjustments over time	Reviewer and approver; focuses on short-term problems; promotes individual solutions to problems
Administration	Not involved	May intervene to influence implementation or service delivery	Overseer	Ombudsman; attempts to promote responsiveness to citizens	Ombudsman, but oversight is constrained by mayor's power; secures services for constituents

	Appointer of manager	Appointer or supervisor of manager; influences key staff appointments	Appointer or appraiser of manager	Appointer or appraiser of manager; proposes changes in management philosophy or practices; seeks to have input on key staff appointments and staff performance	May have role in appointment of CAO, otherwise little involvement; seeks to have input on key staff appointments and staff performance but little impact
Management					
Executive manager or mayor influence and roles	Manager has very high influence relative to council; policy developer and implementer	Manager has much less influence than council; policy adviser and implementer	Manager has high influence; policy proposer and implementer	Manager has high influence; goal proposer and policy initiator (if council does not create a policy framework) and policy proposer and implementer	Elected executive mayor has very high influence; goal and policy initiator and implementer; may delegate administrative assignments to CAO

activists, particularly greater policy initiation on the part of council members and a stronger ombudsman orientation to constituents.

There are many positive aspects to the emerging activist orientation of the council position, but there are shortcomings as well. The council does not necessarily create a clear policy framework, nor does it commit itself to broad goals, and approval of policies may be cautious as the members reserve the option of making policy adjustments over time. Their activity may focus on initiating projects, solving problems, helping constituents, and getting responses to specific shortcomings in administrative performance. Although highly involved in representing citizens, these councils may be weak as collegial and deliberative bodies—to use legislative characteristics described by Vogelsang-Coombs.[8]

With council members acting as a board of activists, there is a prospect for both greater democratic accountability and more direct representation of constituencies but weaker democratic governance than with a board of governors. The city council sets less direction but maintains more immediate control over policy and service delivery and more actively gives voice to citizen concerns. To keep the city moving forward purposefully, the board of activists may need to be guided by a mayor who effectively offers facilitative leadership, or supported by a city manager who helps set the course and keeps the organization on that course. In a sense, this board is more dependent on the city manager for policy direction at the same time that it gives the manager more policy assignments and is more critical of the manager for lapses that occur in the performance of administrative staff.

Implications for Council-Manager Government

Assessment of recent developments in city government suggests that the board of governors type of council is being replaced at least to some extent with the board of activists model. From the perspective of democratic governance and accountability, this shift, with an increasing overlap in the roles of council and manager, has some positive consequences. Elected officials are more active in setting the agenda of short-term policy making, and there is more give and take between the council and manager in considering options. Council members are more skeptical of proposals from staff than in the past. In this respect and in others, council members are demonstrating a more critical orientation toward the manager and staff as well as being more active as policy proponents and ombudsmen. There is closer surveillance of implementation and more adjustment to meet changing circumstances and political realities. Accountability for service delivery is becoming more direct as council members, particularly those elected from districts, see themselves as the agents of individual citizens and groups addressing specific concerns. A wider range of management approaches is now being considered as the council pushes the manager to entertain options involving privatization and introduction of competition—measures that the managers might not have espoused on their own.

There are negative consequences to these changes as well. The city manager is shouldering more of the responsibility for initiating goals and maintaining coherence in governance. This shift reduces democratic control over the direction of the city on the part of council members who viewed themselves as representatives of broad constituencies. Frequent policy adjustments reduce constancy and increase the influence of special interests, even though they increase flexibility and democratic control. Consistency of administrative action may be decreased, whether by more council involvement in implementing decisions or by less council involvement in oversight.

These changes to the board of governors model reflect a shift in attitude on the part of both elected officials and the city manager. Elected officials have a new attitude about what it means to represent their constituents and oversee administrators that is closer to the approach of the board of delegates. Although these council members still believe they should chart the long-term course for their community, the pressing responsibility to assist and respond to constituents often pushes aside a broader focus and attention to long-range concerns. The council member often takes a policy approach that is hands-on and more reactive and focused on responding to current problems than proactive and long-term. The city manager pursues the traditional policy formulating role more actively to fill the vacuum of broad, forward-looking policy leadership that the manager perceives and that elected officials implicitly acknowledge. One manager who worked with a council whose members were limited to two two-year terms suggested that managers had the choice of articulating long-term plans, which made them vulnerable to opposition, or else incorporating the elements that contributed to plans in other policies and budget provisions. Although he did not conceal the plans, he presented them in a way that did not attract attention.

Thus, although both the board of governors and board of activists models for a council offer advantages over the trustee, director, and delegate models, they each have some potential shortcomings. Governors may have some of the remoteness and excessive deference to the city manager that is clearly present among trustees. In a large and highly diverse city of any size, the governor orientation may not provide the active linkage with government that citizens demand. On the other hand, activists may have some of the reactive qualities and narrow focus of delegates.

There have been a number of criticisms of council-manager government in recent years that can be attributed to the shift toward the activist role and the weakening of the governing role by the council. Fragmentation of the city council into a collection of individual members who have difficulty coming to agreement is more likely if the activist approach is the prevailing orientation on a city council. It can be difficult for the activist council to govern, which becomes impossible if the members of the council constantly quarrel with each other. The basic contention of advocates for charter revision in Cincinnati in 1999 was that the council was immobilized by internal dissension. The question "Who's in charge?"[9] probably did not arise often when there was coherent policy direction coming from the mayor and council acting as a board of governors. As we will see later in this article, some contend that the absence of policy coherence creates the need for strengthening the mayor or shifting executive authority from the manager to the mayor.

These changes raise a fundamental question: Can the council-manager form function properly if the city council does not act as a board of governors? There are two aspects to this question. The first concerns whether the council is filling its proper democratic role; the second concerns whether the manager is playing too large a role when compensating for the shortcomings of an activist board. As council members get actively involved in addressing constituency complaints, they become more focused on administrative rather than policy matters. This results in the council having a more limited contribution to determining goals and policies than democratic control would require. Furthermore, it produces tension and interference in the administrative performance of the city. Questions of accountability in dealing with performance problems could arise as mixed accountability to elected ombudsmen and administrative superiors weakens accountability overall.

A remedy for the lack of policy coherence and for confused coordination with staff may be to strengthen the mayor's office in the council-manager form. There are special powers and provisions associated with an empowered mayor in a council-manager form of government. Among the special responsibilities and status of the mayor are the following:

- The mayor delivers the state-of-the-city address.
- The mayor receives a higher salary than council members do.
- The mayor enjoys staff support and the authority to select staff.
- The mayor reviews and comments on the budget of the city manager.

There are changes in authority vis-à-vis the city council:

- The power to veto legislation
- Appointment of council chairs and committee members
- Authority to assign matters to committee
- Nomination of city manager to the council

There are changes in authority vis-à-vis the manager:

- The mayor has the sole authority to initiate removal of the city manager with the approval of council, as well as greater weight in voting to retain the manager.
- The mayor has authority to revise the manager's budget before it is submitted to the council.

These changes, however, raise two related questions that build on the basic issue of whether the board of governors is essential to viable council-manager government. First, can an empowered mayor foster the board of governors model and counter the possibility that a board of activists will fracture? Second, can the council-manager form function properly if the mayor plays too large a role? An enhanced mayor may ignore the team building aspects of the position and become the "activist-in-chief" who uses a favorable position to push a personal agenda, ignoring the rest of the council. An empowered mayor may expect the manager to act as the mayor's agent rather than to serve the entire council. The changes in authority vis-à-vis the manager listed above seem particular likely to have these effects of aligning the manager closely with the mayor. Other council members may perceive that the mayor is overshadowing them and seek to curtail his or her success.

The endemic disagreement about the scope of their respective positions that exists among elected officials in mayor-council governments may become a persistent issue in council-manager governments as well. If the response to dissension among council members focuses entirely on increasing the power position of the mayor, the logical conclusion may be an effort to change the form of government itself. Although there are distinctive features and potential strengths of the mayor-council form, adopting this form is not recommended as the most efficacious way for a council-manager government to deal with internal dissension on the council and to restore the positive combination of political and professional leadership that this form is uniquely capable of achieving. The mayor-council form is centered on executive political leadership in which the emphasis on professionalism is variable (although typically high) and the council is likely to act in the constrained manner typical of a board of delegates. In view of the formal and political resources of the mayor, it is difficult for the council in a mayor-council city to move beyond a delegate orientation with its emphasis on representation alone rather than on representation and governance.

Fostering a Composite Model for the Council

As a way of combining the benefits of both approaches, a composite model of activist-governor may be a new ideal. There is some evidence that it is possible to achieve and maintain a board of activist governors; many councils may already be demonstrating this combination. In such cities, activism is incorporated into council behavior without producing dissension and undermining cohesion. Council members balance their interest in pressing concerns with recognition of the need to look beyond the scope of their own term of office. They act on behalf of citizens to help resolve problems with city government and seek to secure services for constituents without either becoming preoccupied with complaint handling or inclined to interfere in the specifics of management and service delivery. In the survey of city managers conducted in 1997, most managers considered both elected officials and themselves to have high influence on policy making as noted previously (see note 2). The managers indicated that the council was extensively involved in efforts to resolve complaints for citizens in 58 percent of the cities where the council had greater influence and 55 percent of the cities with equal influence, compared with 44 percent when the manager had greater influence. Furthermore, when elected official influence was higher, 47 percent sought to secure services for constituents compared to 36 percent when influence was equal and 34 percent when the manager's influence was greater. It appears that the greater the influence of the council, the more likely it is that activist tendencies are present.

What impact does higher activism have on the council-manager relationship? Among managers with more influential and activist council members, 22 percent reported a serious problem with unclear division of labor between the council and manager, compared to 9 percent experiencing this problem when influence was equal and 7 percent when the manager's influence was greater. Thus, it appears that although an activist orientation combined with higher council influence produces a higher level of confusion about respective contributions, this is not a widespread problem. In more than three-quarters of these cities, there is still a reasonably clear division of labor. In these cities, an activist-governor combination appears to be present and is working.

In the minority of cities in which there are disagreements about respective roles and activism may be undercutting governance, certain steps might be taken to promote balance between activism and governance. First, the concurrent needs for leadership and teamwork within the council can be addressed. The structural changes outlined earlier that affect the mayor's status and authority vis-à-vis the council can be made to strengthen the mayor while still reinforcing a facilitative approach to leadership. These changes would increase the capability of the mayor to pull—even push—the council together while respecting the contributions of members.

There are two major reasons for increasing the mayor's authority. The manager is not able to achieve cohesion on a fragmented council (although the manager can encourage and reinforce it). Furthermore, the manager should not be shaping the vision of the city (as opposed to helping the council as it shapes the vision). The mayor should be able to take the lead in promoting common goals if the council is not able to find cohesion on its own. If mayors, however, come to depend on enhanced powers, they could easily wind up going their own way and alienating their councils. The purpose of increasing the mayor's stature and authority—promoting cohesive leadership—is undermined by the corrective measures. The formally empowered mayor is an insurance policy in case no other means are available to bring the council together to function as a whole. The mayor's council leadership goal should be, however, to restore collective leadership, not to seek to increase his or her capacity to act alone. Furthermore, the structural changes that alter the authority of the mayor vis-à-vis the city manager should be avoided because they are likely to promote disagreement between the mayor and council rather than overcome it.

Second, a mayor-led council team can seek to blend the best of the governor and activist models. The council should be selective in setting goals. It should set goals for at least the most important aspects of local government in a given community even if it cannot establish and pursue a comprehensive set of goals. The intent of this proposal is not to suggest that councils should limit the scope of their goal setting. Rather, it is based on recognition that other pressures interfere with a council's ability to establish a complete mission for the city. It is preferable to identify which policy areas are most important or which problems are most critical and establish goals in those areas rather than to allow goal setting to be done by default or to fail to develop any over-arching goals at all.

The approach to oversight is similar. The council can identify critical areas in which it monitors results. Finally, the council should take advantage of the key feature of the council-manager form: its ability to choose the executive who best matches the city's needs and circumstances and to hold the city manager continuously accountable for his or her performance. The activist-governor council would have a systematic process for evaluating the manager's performance and would extend the evaluation to assessing how well the manager is supervising the performance of department heads and other key staff members.

The council should also make other contributions that are natural to activists: identify current issues and problems and propose ways to deal with them, ensure that policy decisions are acceptable to voters, making certain that citizens are treated responsively and responsibly as the city implements policy and delivers services, and inject new ideas about how the city might do its work. The mayor and council on a board of activist governors pay attention to the direction and pace of city government action and also attend to the pressing needs of their constituents.

Conclusion

Structure and performance interact. Form of government and method of electing the mayor and council members affect which roles council members can choose, but their attitude and behavior affect how they perform and the roles they wind up filling. Council members in a council-manager city are "permitted" by the form to have a number of options. If they allow the manager to essentially run city government, they can become trustees who react to the manager's initiative. If they exploit their formal power over the manager to not only determine policy but also insert themselves in the administrative process, they can be directors who undermine the professional dimension of city government. They can seek to attain the traditional ideal in this form and be governors who set a framework of policy goals in close cooperation with the manager, oversee how well the policies developed to meet goals are accomplishing their objectives, and hold the manager accountable for how well city government is performing. Finally, they can be activists who take a hands-on approach to setting the agenda of city government and acting on behalf of citizens, but in the process give less attention to their governance responsibilities.

Presumably, district and partisan elections and term limits reinforce the activist approach. Strengthening the mayor may be a structural change that offsets the tendency of some activist boards to be fragmented. Still, structure does not fully explain approach. Council members' political context, their attitudes about holding office, and their capabilities produce variations within the same combination of structures.

Elected officials in a mayor-council government have difficulty filling any of these roles if the mayor is formally strong and the administrative structure is oriented fully to the mayor in its performance. The council members individually and collectively tend to be delegates who present policy preferences that reflect the sentiments of their constituents and ombudsmen who seek to assist constituents with problems. Having a chief administrative officer whose appointment is approved by the council can increase the extent to which the top administrator feels accountable to both the mayor and the council in his or her policy formulation and administrative direction. With support from a chief administrative officer, the council may be able to approach the impact that activists have on policy decisions and administrative performance and strengthen their contributions to governance.

In a council-manager city, the council can determine its own orientation with the support of the city manager. It is clear that council members are choosing to bring greater activism to the position and demonstrate a more hands-on approach to solving current problems and are more likely to act as ombudsmen for constituents—the characteristics of a delegate council. They may also choose to maintain some of the contributions that the board of governors council has made. With a combined activist-governor approach, they can be partners with the city manager in shaping the direction and programs of city government along with doing more to represent citizens in articulating policy demands and seeking better services from administrative staff. Council members in a mayor-council city may wish to shift in the opposite way, preserving their strong commitment to representation while becoming more active contributors to the policy-making process. In both cases, the form of government constrains but does not determine the behavior of council members.

Notes

1. Woodruff, C. R. (ed.). *A New Municipal Program*. New York: D. Appleton, 1919, p. 37.

2. The survey was conducted in 1997 by the Public Administration Program, North Carolina State University, with the assistance of the International City/County Management Association (ICMA) in selecting the sample. The sample was drawn from cities that had an appointed administrative officer, with all cities over fifty thousand in population included and a one-quarter random sample of cities between twenty-five hundred and fifty thousand population.

The response rate was 59 percent. The number of respondents from council-manager cities was 485.

3. This and the following sections are adapted from Svara, J. H. "Representation and Governance: Redefining Roles for Large Council-Manager Cities in the United States." In N. Rao (ed.), *Representation and Community in Western Democracies*. London: Macmillan, 2000.

4. Svara, J. H. "The Myth of the Dichotomy: Complementarity of Politics and Administration in the Past and Future of Public Administration." *Public Administration Review*, 2001, *61*, 176–183.

5. When comparing the combined influence for budgeting and economic development policy making, in 18 percent of cases elected officials had slightly more influence than the city manager, in 34 percent the influence was equal, and in 36 percent the manager had slightly more influence than the elected officials. The influence rating was a five-point scale from very low to very high. The slight difference is one point on the scale.

6. Svara, J. H. "The Shifting Boundary Between Elected Officials and City Managers in Large Council-Manager Cities." *Public Administration Review*, 1999, *59*, 44–53.

7. The broker role is not new (see, for example the 1979 ICMA publication "New Worlds of Service," published in Washington, D.C.), but it appears to apply to a broader range of activities than in the past.

8. Vogelsang-Coombs, V. "Inside an American City Council: Democracy, Leadership and Governance." Paper prepared for annual conference of the PA Theory Network, Leiden, Holland, June 2001.

9. Gurwitt, R. "Nobody in Charge." *Governing*, 1997, *12*, 20–24.

James H. Svara is professor in and head of the Department of Political Science and Public Administration, North Carolina State University; he is a member of the Model Charter Revision Committee.

An Institutionalist Perspective on Mayoral Leadership: Linking Leadership Style to Formal Structure

Craig M. Wheeland

The factors that influence effective mayoral leadership are still not well understood. There is continuing debate in the academic literature over theories of mayoral leadership,[1] and many communities debate ways to change their form of government to influence how their mayor provides leadership. In this essay, I use James March and Johann Olsen's institutionalist theory of politics to guide my interpretation of how the formal structure of municipal government can influence mayoral leadership style.[2] I refine James Svara's two models of mayoral leadership—the executive mayor and the facilitative mayor—to describe the styles supported by the formal rules found in the charters or statutes used in the forty largest cities in the United States.[3] Three facilitative mayor subtypes (council leader, community leader, and partial executive) and four executive mayor subtypes (strong leader, constrained leader, legislative leader, and weak leader) can be identified and ranked according to the formal resources available to support their efforts. These findings have implications for the practice of city politics and for the development of a theory of mayoral leadership.

An Institutionalist Theory of Mayoral Leadership

March and Olsen suggest that "political institutions define the framework within which politics takes place."[4] They argue that rules are the means by which an institution affects behavior. Rules are the "routines, procedures, conventions, roles, strategies, organizational forms, and technologies around which activity is constructed."[5] Rules also include the "beliefs, paradigms, codes, cultures, and knowledge that surround, support, elaborate, and contradict those roles and routines."[6] They explain that rules "define relationships among roles in terms of what an incumbent of one role owes to incumbents of other roles."[7] They argue that the "logic of appropriateness associated with obligatory action" shapes how individuals follow the rules supported by the political institutions in which they work.[8] In other words, an official shapes his or her action by defining the situation, determining his or her role, assessing the appropriateness of different actions in the situation, and carrying out the most appropriate one.[9]

Of course, discretion exists in using rules, because they are not monolithic and may be contradictory and ambiguous, so conformity to as well as deviation from rules can occur in a political institution. They conclude that trust, "a confidence that appropriate behavior can be expected most of the time," supports the network of rules and rule-bound relations.[10] Deviation from the rules (violating the "logic of appropriateness") undermines trust among officials and potentially erodes support for the political institution as well.

Research on mayoral leadership recognizes the contextual relevance of the municipal institution, although the relative weight given to institutional features varies among scholars. Svara has developed a theory of mayoral leadership that emphasizes the formal institutions of government.[11] He argues theories of mayoral leadership should begin with "the form of government in which the mayor's office is located," because the form of city government defines the basic "roles and types of leadership" to be offered by the mayor.[12] He suggests that the two main forms of city government (strong mayor–council and council-manager) establish the formal preconditions for mayoral leadership styles—an executive-style leader and a facilitative-style leader, respectively. He argues that a mayor increases the chances of being successful if he or she adopts a leadership style compatible with the form of city government in which the mayor serves.

The implication here is clear: using a particular form of government creates a set of institutions whose formal rules can structure behavior in the ways March and Olsen suggest. Although it is possible for a mayor to use a leadership style different from the one supported by the formal rules, doing so may violate the logic of appropriateness and potentially erode the trust that supports the formal institutions in the city's political system.

Svara based his model of the executive mayor on mayors in forms of government marked by the principle of separation of powers, as in a strong mayor–council city. This principle is the foundation for a conflict pattern of interaction among officials, especially elected officials, who have incentive to compete with one another to accomplish their agendas. Svara suggests that "by establishing direction, forging coalitions, galvanizing the bureaucracy—in general by managing and resolving conflict in all dimensions of the governmental process—the Executive Mayor becomes the driving force in this form of government."[13] Indeed, the successful executive mayor draws power from formal and informal sources to become the dominant actor in city government.

Svara's facilitative mayor model is based on governmental forms marked by the unification-of-powers principle, such as the council-manager city, in which the city council has the legislative and executive powers of government.

This principle is the foundation for a cooperative pattern of interaction among elected and appointed officials (the city manager being an example of the latter). The facilitative mayor has ample authority to act as the "guiding force in city government who helps insure that all other officials are performing as well as possible and that all are moving in the right direction."[14] Like the executive mayor, the facilitative mayor can act as a "policy initiator," helping to set the agenda and develop policies to address problems facing the community.[15] However, the facilitative mayor need not pyramid resources to be successful. Instead, he or she "accomplishes objectives through enhancing the efforts of others. . . . Rather than seeking power as the way to accomplish tasks, the facilitative mayor seeks to empower others."[16]

The research presented here builds on Svara's work in two ways. First, since the particular formal powers of a mayor can vary within each form of government, it is possible to refine Svara's models by identifying subtypes of executive and facilitative mayors. Second, it is possible to link other formal institutional features, such as full-time status of the mayor and design of the electoral system, to Svara's theory to develop a more complete institutionalist perspective on mayoral leadership.

Types of Mayoral Leadership

There are twenty-six mayor-council cities, thirteen council-manager cities, and one commission city (Portland, Oregon) among the forty largest cities in the United States.[17] All forty mayors have the formal power to perform ceremonial activities, which gives them the opportunity to cultivate a positive image with the public. Aside from this common feature, the form of government used in each city creates rules that serve as an incentive for a leadership style. Using Svara's two models of mayoral leadership, the twenty-six mayor-council cities generally support an executive mayor, and the thirteen council-manager cities along with the commission city generally support a facilitative mayor. Within these two basic types of mayoral leadership, additional distinctions can be made to refine Svara's classification. These subtypes capture the variation in key formal institutional features affecting the ability of the mayor to perform as an executive or as a facilitator.

Facilitative Mayor. Interpretation of the data on the thirteen council-manager cities and one commission city presented in Table 1 suggests three types of facilitative mayor: council leader (CL), community leader (CML), and partial executive (PE). The CL (as an example, San Antonio) is defined as a mayor who is a voting member of the council and the presiding officer at council meetings. The CML (as in San Diego) is distinguished from the CL by a charter provision that empowers the mayor to present a legislative program addressing the needs of the city (that is, an annual state-of-the-city speech) or by the power to review and comment on the budget prepared by the city manager before it is submitted to the council (the "first review" power). The PE is

Table 1. Facilitative Mayors

City	Formal Institutional Features						Type of Mayoral Leader
	Member of Council	Votes with Council	Presiding Officer	Proposes Legislation	General Veto Power	Prepares Budget	
Oklahoma City	yes	yes	yes	no	no	no	Council leader
Austin	yes	yes	yes	no	no	no	Council leader
San Antonio	yes	yes	yes	no	no	no	Council leader
Virginia Beach	yes	yes	yes	no	no	no	Council leader
Fort Worth	yes	yes	yes	no	no	no	Council leader
San Diego	yes	yes	yes	yes	no	no	Community leader
Dallas	yes	yes	yes	yes	no	no	Community leader
Tucson	yes	yes	yes	yes	no	no	Community leader
Phoenix	yes	yes	yes	yes	no	no	Community leader
Charlotte	no[1]	no[2]	yes	yes	yes	no	Partial executive
Portland	yes	yes	yes	no	no	yes[3]	Partial executive
Long Beach	yes	no	yes	yes	yes	no[4]	Partial executive
San Jose	yes	yes	yes	yes	no	yes[5]	Partial executive
Kansas City	yes	yes	yes	yes	yes	no[6]	Partial executive

Notes:

1. The mayor is not formally a member of the council primarily because of voting status and administrative prerogatives.

2. The mayor does not vote with the council except for three decision types: to break ties, on the appointment or dismissal of the city manager, and on controversial amendments to the zoning ordinance.

3. The mayor usually is the commissioner in charge of the office of finance and administration. The mayor then may appoint the city's financial officer and direct the budget process. Indeed, during the budget process all departments are brought back into the mayor's portfolio.

4. The city manager is responsible for preparing the budget and submitting it to the mayor, who then submits the budget to the council; however, the mayor may attach comments, recommendations, and amendments to the budget for the council to consider.

5. The mayor initiates the budget process. The mayor's budget director and staff work with the city manager's budget director and staff to prepare the budget. Any differences are worked out before the budget is submitted to the council. The mayor is recognized as the leader in budgetary matters, which is an understanding firmly grounded in the formal language used in the charter; therefore differences are usually resolved to reflect the mayor's priorities. Note that this is different from the first-review approach used in Kansas City and Long Beach.

6. The city manager prepares the budget and submits it to the mayor for first review. The mayor forwards the budget to the council along with a letter of transmittal in which the mayor discusses his or her recommendations and endorsements.

a facilitative mayor who has one or more powers of the executive mayor, such as veto power (Charlotte, Long Beach, and Kansas City) or the power to prepare the budget (Portland and San Jose). Of the fourteen cities with facilitative mayors, five have CLs, four have CMLs, and five have PEs.

On the basis of the extent to which the institutional design supports facilitative leadership, the CMLs are most likely to be successful, followed by the CLs and then the PEs.[18] The CML may find it easier than the CL to draw attention to specific problems facing the city, offer a proposed course of action, and influence allocation of resources in the budget because these are charter-based responsibilities. The power to propose a legislative program or first-review the city manager's budget allows the mayor to provide leadership without necessarily undermining the prerogatives of the council or the city manager; indeed, it can enhance the mayor's ability to guide the policy-making process. Of course, mayors may choose to offer a state-of-the-city speech, undertake efforts to offer a legislative program, and influence budgetary priorities even if they do not have a charter-based responsibility to do so (as in the case of San Antonio). If the practice becomes routine and part of the informal set of expectations (that is, "informal" rules), then the CL can be just as successful a facilitative mayor as the CML.

The PE has greater obstacles to overcome than the CL in performing as a facilitative-style leader. The power to veto ordinances, or to initiate the budget process and prepare the budget, creates rules more appropriate for an executive style of leadership. Because the PE's role is not clearly defined as a guiding force, the PE's actions could produce tension and conflict among council members and appointed officials rather than promote cooperation and teamwork. Salary, appointment powers, reporting responsibility, and the electoral system are other formal institutional features that also can affect how these three types of facilitative mayor perform.

The mayors' salaries can influence the amount of time the official is willing and financially able to devote to duties. The salaries vary from part-time (Oklahoma City pays $2,000 per year) to half-time (Austin pays $35,000 per year) and full-time (San Jose pays $87,550 per year). The full-time salaries offered in Kansas City (PE), San Diego (CML), Long Beach (PE), Portland (PE), and San Jose (PE) are for these mayors a formal incentive to spend most of their time performing their duties. Half-time mayors, as in Austin (CL), Virginia Beach (CL), Tucson (CML), and Phoenix (CML); and part-time mayors, in Oklahoma City (CL), San Antonio (CL), Fort Worth (CL), Dallas (CML), and Charlotte (PE), lack this incentive.

Appointing the members of boards, commissions, and authorities, as well as being permitted to appoint assistants to form a mayoral staff, can increase the potential of a facilitative mayor to emerge as a guiding force in city politics.[19] The power to appoint members of boards, commissions, and authorities enhances the mayor's status as the official with the best opportunity to establish relationships with the city's public, private, and nonprofit leadership.

The power to appoint assistants who work on policy and management topics increases the mayor's ability to influence policy and coordinate council members and the city manager.

In twelve of the fourteen cities with facilitative mayors, the mayor has at least one of the two types of appointment power. In nine of the twelve cities—Oklahoma City (CL), San Diego (CML), Tucson (CML), Phoenix (CML), Charlotte (PE), Long Beach (PE), Portland (PE), Kansas City (PE), and San Jose (PE)—the mayor has both types of appointment power. For example, San Diego's mayor has the most extensive appointment power of any facilitative mayor: she appoints members of some boards, commissions, and authorities with council approval and appoints thirty staff members, eight of whom work on policy and management topics. San Antonio (CL) and Dallas (CML) are the only two cities that permit the mayor to appoint citizens to serve on some boards, commissions, and authorities, but not to appoint assistants. Austin (CL) is the only city that permits the mayor to appoint assistants, but not members of boards and commissions. Austin's mayor appoints four staff members, two of whom work on policy and management topics. Only the mayors in Virginia Beach and Fort Worth have neither appointment power.

Having a charter-based responsibility to prepare reports and submit them to the council can also increase the potential for the facilitative mayor to emerge as a guiding force in city politics. This power to report enhances the mayor's opportunity to set the public agenda via press conferences, council meetings, and various appearances before community groups. Of course, a mayor may prepare reports and submit them to the council and to the public even if there is no official responsibility, but the seriousness with which these reports are received may be less than if the mayor routinely did so as part of his or her official duties. None of the charters in the five cities with CLs grant the mayor this power. The mayors in two of the four cities with CMLs (Tucson and Phoenix) and three of the five cities with PEs (Charlotte, Portland, and San Jose) have formal reporting responsibilities.

In twelve of fourteen cities with a facilitative mayor, two of the four features found in electoral systems—direct election and nonpartisan election—support the mayor as a guiding force in city politics. All fourteen cities permit direct election of the mayor by the voters, and in all but Tucson (CML) and Charlotte (PE) elections are nonpartisan. Direct election gives a facilitative mayor the visibility in the community and contact with voters across the city needed to build an electoral coalition that supports his or her efforts to work as a guiding force once in office. Nonpartisan election is also compatible with an effort to work as a guiding force, rather than a driving force, although there may be some undesirable effects, such as low voter turnout, a middle-class or business bias, low-quality policy debates, and a high rate of reelection for the incumbent.[20] The main advantage of a nonpartisan election is not having to engage voters initially as a Democrat, Republican, or other party's candidate. The opportunity exists, therefore, to create an identity that, at the very least, appeals beyond party labels and supports a mayoral candidate's effort to build an inclusive electoral coalition.

Two other features of electoral systems, the length of the mayor's term and term limits, vary across the fourteen cities. A mayor who serves a longer term and who can seek reelection to more than two terms has the potential to nurture relationships with voters, other public officials, and interest group leaders, all of which enables the mayor to emerge as the guiding force in city politics. Two of the five CLs (Oklahoma City and Virginia Beach), two of the four CMLs (Tucson and Phoenix), and one of the five PEs (Portland) serve four-year terms without a limit on the number of terms served. These six mayors enjoy a formal advantage over other facilitative mayors with shorter terms or who are limited to two terms.

Consideration of additional formal institutional features—salary, appointment powers, reporting responsibilities, and the electoral system—complicates the effort to rank mayors because their use varies widely. Rather than attempt to assess the myriad combinations of these features in all fifteen cities, for each type of facilitative mayor I offer a profile of one who is advantaged by these additional formal features:

- Among the CMLs, the mayor of San Diego is well positioned to be successful because he or she earns a full-time salary; serves a four-year term; and has the power to appoint members of boards, commissions, and authorities (without council approval) as well as assistants (without council approval).
- Among the CLs, the mayor of Austin is well positioned to be successful because he or she earns a half-time salary and has the power to appoint assistants (without council approval).
- Among the PEs serving in council-manager cities, the mayor of Kansas City is well positioned to be successful because he or she earns a full-time salary; serves a four-year term; has the power to appoint members of boards, commissions, and authorities (without council approval) and assistants as well (without council approval).

Fort Worth's (CL) mayor is least advantaged of the fourteen cities when considering these additional features, because he or she receives part-time pay, serves a two-year term, and does not have either formal appointment powers or formal reporting responsibility.

The complete set of formal features used in Charlotte (PE) place its mayor in the least favorable position to emerge as a guiding force. Charlotte's mayor is part-time, serves a two-year term, is elected in a partisan election, may vote with the council only in rare circumstances, has a general veto power (one of only three mayors out of the fourteen to have this power), may be "active in enforcing the law," may require members of city departments to meet with him or her for consultation and advice, and may hire "experts to examine the affairs of any department." This combination of institutional features increases the potential for a conflict pattern to emerge between the mayor and Charlotte's other officials (council members and the city manager), in part because of the ambiguity in the rules defining the mayor's role. Following the logic of appropriateness is difficult for all PEs, but especially for Charlotte's mayor.

Executive Mayor. Interpretation of the data on the twenty-six mayor-council cities presented in Table 2 suggests four types of executive mayor: strong leader (SL), constrained leader (CSL), legislative leader (LL), and weak leader (WL). All twenty-six mayors have the power to propose legislation; submit reports on their government's performance; execute the law; appoint assistants (only Indianapolis requires council approval of these appointments); and appoint many, if not all, members of boards, commissions, and authorities (in some cities, without council approval). Five other formal powers that vary across the twenty-six cities are used to distinguish the four types of executive mayor: presiding at council meetings, vetoing ordinances, preparing the budget, appointing department heads, and appointing a chief administrative officer (CAO). The SL (New York, for instance) is defined as a mayor who prepares the budget, who can veto ordinances, and who appoints department heads (and in some cities a CAO) without council approval.

The CSL (as in the case of Baltimore) is distinguished from the SL by the requirement that appointment of department heads (and in some cities the CAO) must be approved by the council (in St. Louis, the mayor's power to prepare the budget is constrained by the existence of a board of estimate and apportionment). The LL is distinguished by serving as presiding officer at council meetings and having the power either to vote as a member of the council (Houston) or to vote under special circumstances such as to break a tie (El Paso and Chicago). The WL is distinguished by using boards and commissions to appoint some department heads, especially key department heads such as the police chief (Los Angeles) and fire chief (Milwaukee). Of the twenty-six cities with executive mayors, nine have SLs, twelve have CSLs, three have LLs, and two have WLs.

On the basis of the extent to which the institutional design supports exercising executive-style leadership, SLs are more likely to succeed than the other mayoral types, especially WLs.[21] The SLs' appointment powers give them formal control over the executive branch, which can help them emerge as the driving force in city government. As presiding officer of the council, an LL may find it easier to influence the council's agenda and development of policy in comparison to the other types of executive mayor, especially if the LL also has veto power (El Paso and Chicago). Yet all three LLs, like CSLs, appoint department heads with council approval, which potentially reduces their control over the executive branch. The WLs face the greatest institutional obstacles to becoming the driving force in part because boards and commissions are given direct authority over some department heads. Therefore, the rank order of mayors from highest to lowest is (1) SLs, (2) LLs with a veto power, (3) CSLs, (4) LLs who lack a veto power (Houston), and (5) WLs. Two other formal institutional features—salary and the electoral system—may also affect whether any of these subtypes of executive mayor emerges as the driving force in city politics.

In twenty-five of the twenty-six cities with executive mayors, the mayor earns a full-time salary, ranging from $75,000 in Nashville to $170,000 in Chicago. The full-time status of these twenty-five mayors gives them the formal incentive to devote the time needed to emerge as the driving force in their cities. This is not the case for El Paso's mayor, an LL who earns a half-time salary.

All twenty-six mayors are directly elected by the voters and all but two serve a four-year term; the mayors in Houston and El Paso serve two-year terms. The same rationale supporting direct election of a facilitative mayor holds for election of an executive mayor. Direct election bestows on them the visibility in the community and the contact with all voters across the city needed to build an electoral coalition that supports his or her effort to emerge, in this case, as a driving force.

Two other electoral features vary across the twenty-six cities: term limits and partisan elections. Mayors in fourteen cities have term limits, which is a disadvantage in comparison to the other mayors who can extend their influence over a longer period of time. Mayors in eleven of the fourteen cities are limited to two terms: New York (SL), Philadelphia (SL), New Orleans (SL), Denver (SL), Atlanta (CSL), Jacksonville (CSL), Albuquerque (CSL), Oakland (CSL), San Francisco (CSL), Washington (CSL), and Los Angeles (WL). The mayors of Nashville (SL) and Houston (LL) are limited to three terms, and the mayor of El Paso (LL) is limited to four terms. Houston and El Paso's mayors serve two-year terms, so they are limited to a maximum of six and eight years, respectively. Partisan elections are used in only seven cities: two have SLs (Philadelphia and New York) and five have CSLs (Baltimore, Indianapolis, St. Louis, Pittsburgh, and Washington). These seven mayors can use the political party as a means to contest an election, shape a legislative program, and organize government so that they become the driving force in governing the city.

Consideration of the mayor's salary and the design of the electoral system suggests how to refine the ranking of executive mayors. The mayors serving in Baltimore, Indianapolis, St. Louis, and Pittsburgh (all CSLs) are advantaged by these other formal features, because they earn a full-time salary, serve a four-year term without term limits, and are elected in a partisan election. If one discounts the impact of being limited to two four-year terms, then the mayors of New York (SL), Philadelphia (SL), and Washington (CSL) could be added to this list of advantaged mayors. The mayor of Los Angeles, already disadvantaged by being a WL, also is disadvantaged by the use of nonpartisan elections and term limits. El Paso's mayor is most disadvantaged by these other formal features, because the mayor is an LL who earns a half-time salary, serves a two-year term with a four-term limit, and is elected in a nonpartisan election.

Table 2. Executive Mayors

City	Formal Institutional Features					Type of Mayoral Leader
	Presiding Officer	General Veto Power	Prepares Budget	Appoints Department Heads Without Council	Appoints CAO Without Council	
Philadelphia	no	yes	yes	yes[1]	yes	Strong leader
New York	no	yes	yes	yes	yes	Strong leader
Nashville	no	yes	yes	yes[2]	n/a	Strong leader
Boston	no	yes	yes	yes	yes	Strong leader
Detroit	no	yes	yes	yes	n/a	Strong leader
New Orleans	no	yes	yes	yes[3]	yes	Strong leader
Denver	no	yes	yes	yes	n/a	Strong leader
Columbus	no	yes	yes	yes	n/a	Strong leader
Cleveland	no	yes	yes	yes	n/a	Strong leader
Memphis	no	yes	yes	no	no	Constrained leader
Atlanta	no	yes	yes	no	no	Constrained leader
Jacksonville	no	yes	yes	no	yes	Constrained leader
Seattle	no	yes	yes	no[4]	n/a	Constrained leader
Pittsburgh	no	yes	yes	no	n/a	Constrained leader
Baltimore	no	yes	yes[5]	no	n/a	Constrained leader
Indianapolis	no	yes	yes	no	n/a	Constrained leader
St. Louis	no	yes	yes[6]	yes	n/a	Constrained leader
Albuquerque	no	yes	yes	no	no	Constrained leader
Oakland	no	yes[7]	yes[8]	no	no	Constrained leader
San Francisco	no	yes	yes	no[9]	no	Constrained leader
Washington	no	yes	yes	no	yes	Constrained leader
El Paso	yes	yes	yes	no	no	Legislative leader
Houston	yes	no	yes	no	yes	Legislative leader

Chicago	yes	yes	yes	no	Legislative leader
Milwaukee	no	yes	yes	no[10]	Weak leader
Los Angeles	no	yes	yes	no[11]	Weak leader

Notes:

1. The mayor appoints the managing director, director of finance, and the city representative without council approval. Other department heads, such as the police commissioner, the fire commissioner, and the recreation commissioner, are appointed by the managing director with the approval of the mayor. By custom, mayors traditionally have exerted control over these appointments.

2. Only the director of finance and the director of law require council approval.

3. The CAO appoints department heads with the mayor's approval.

4. Most appointments require the council's approval.

5. The board of estimate, which consists of the mayor, the council president, the comptroller, the city solicitor, and the director of public works, establishes fiscal policy, so the mayor's power is constrained formally. However, because the mayor appoints the director of public works and the city solicitor, he controls three of the five votes; therefore the budget reflects the mayor's priorities.

6. The board of estimate and apportionment, which consists of the mayor, the comptroller (an elected official), and the council president, prepares the annual budget and submits it to council, so the mayor's budget authority is constrained.

7. Because Measure X, which passed in November 1998, was not clear on how the mayor's new veto power would work, the mayor, city council, and city attorney agreed to follow these procedures: (1) the mayor has no input on resolutions, so a simple majority rules; (2) for an ordinance, the mayor may vote to break a tie; on a five-to-three vote, the mayor has the option of sending the bill back to the council and demanding a six-to-two vote in order to pass.

8. The mayor is "responsible for the submission of an annual budget to the council which shall be prepared by the City Manager under the direction of the Mayor and Council." At the time of the budget submission, the mayor submits a "general statement of the conditions of the affairs of the city, the goals of the administration, and recommendations of such measures as he may deem expedient and proper to accomplish such goals."

9. The mayor appoints and removes a controller with council approval. With the mayor's approval, the city administrator appoints the heads of four departments: administrative services, public works, solid waste, and public guardian and administration. The heads of other departments are appointed by the mayor according to this procedure: boards or commissions, such as the fire commission and the police commission, submit a list of at least three qualified applicants to the mayor, and if the mayor rejects this list, then the board or commission submits another list.

10. The mayor appoints with council approval the commissioners of public works, health, building inspection, city development, and others as well. The major exceptions are the chiefs of police and fire, who are appointed by the fire and police commission. The mayor appoints the members of the fire and police commission, with the council's approval, to staggered five-year terms.

11. In addition to the CAO, the mayor appoints (with council approval) the purchasing agent, treasurer, city clerk, and the director of planning. The mayor appoints with council approval the boards of commissioners that control these departments: airports, harbors, libraries, pensions, recreation and parks, water and power, animal regulation, personnel, fire, police, building and safety city planning, municipal courts, public utilities and transportation, social services, and traffic. Board members serve five-year staggered terms. The mayor, with council approval, appoints a chief administrative officer for each of these departments, except for the chief of police. The mayor appoints, with council approval, the chief of police from a list of qualified candidates prepared by the board of police commissioners.

Implications of This Research for Practice

For those reform-minded political leaders and their supporters who think formal institutional features are preventing their mayor from offering the kind of leadership needed in their city (either the executive or the facilitative style), this research offers two options.

Option one is to change the institutional design to use the strongest version of mayoral leadership appropriate to the form of government and adopt one or more of the other institutional features that enhance the mayor's formal position, such as a full-time salary. For example, in November 1995 San Francisco voters approved Measure E, which altered the city charter by giving the mayor more control over appointing and removing the city administrator and department heads as well as increasing the mayor's influence in the budget process.[22] These changes made San Francisco's mayor a constrained leader rather than a weak leader.

There is, however, a risk in using this option. Some changes may lead to a package of formal institutional features that do not consistently support either the executive or the facilitative style of leadership. For example, giving the mayor a general veto power in a council-manager city (Charlotte, Long Beach, Kansas City) or giving the mayor control over the budget (San Jose) rather than the power of first review (Kansas City) creates rules that are inconsistent with the facilitative style. Similarly, leaving in place rules such as vesting the city manager with the power to appoint department heads inhibits the mayor from developing an executive style of leadership. This lack of consistency in the rules generates ambiguity that can inhibit an official's ability to interpret his or her role. In other words, following the logic of appropriateness is more difficult and the potential to erode trust among officials and with the public increases. As Protasel argues, "injecting the idea of the separation of powers into the council-manager system would seem to put the directly elected mayor on a collision course with both the council and the city manager. Policy-making deadlock—a continual threat in mayor-council systems—could be expected to occur periodically. . . ."[23]

Option two is to change the form of government to create the formal institutional incentives needed for another style of mayoral leadership (executive or facilitative) and pattern of interaction among officials (conflict or cooperation) to emerge. Several of the cities in this study have explored this option in recent decades—San Diego,[24] Kansas City,[25] Dallas,[26] Washington,[27] and Oakland[28]—but these efforts were not fully successful, in part because of voter opposition. Although changing the basic form of government is difficult to accomplish, it is preferable to producing a hybrid set of formal institutional features that inhibit the efforts of all city officials to follow the logic of appropriateness.

Oakland is an example of a city that first pursued option one and then moved on to option two. In 1968–69, Oakland's mayor received a part-time salary and had three secretaries and one administrative assistant, a package,

Pressman felt, that helped explain why the city manager was so dominant in that era.[29] By the 1990s, Oakland's mayor received a full-time salary and could appoint a number of assistants, among them a chief of staff, an assistant for media relations, an assistant for economic development, and an assistant for environmental policy. These changes established formal features that were consistent with the rules supporting a facilitative style of leadership. Yet some city officials, especially the mayors, and community leaders continued to push for changing the mayor's powers. In November 1998, Oakland's voters were asked to approve changes in the mayor's powers that would essentially establish a mayor-council form of government.[30] This time, by a vote of three to one, Measure X passed. The change is not permanent, however. A provision in the measure requires citizens to vote to approve it again in six years or the council-manager form will be restored.

Implications of This Research for Theory

This research suggests how an institutional perspective constitutes a needed foundation for developing a theory of mayoral leadership. By beginning with an institutional perspective, we are more likely to:

- Recognize the two main models of mayoral leadership, the facilitative mayor and the executive mayor
- Develop an appreciation for each style of leadership
- Recognize the subtypes of facilitative and executive mayor
- Understand the impact other institutional features, such as salary and the design of the electoral system, have on mayoral leadership
- Understand how contextual variables (political culture, fiscal resources, economic elite activity, and interest group activity) and proximate variables (the mayor's skills, personality, vision of the job, and legislative program) combine with formal institutional features to affect a mayor's performance

Regarding this last point, the mayors of San Diego and Philadelphia have the formal institutional features needed to be successful facilitative and executive mayors, respectively; yet whether they are successful depends on the influence of the other contextual variables and proximate variables.

Finally, this analysis suggests five questions to guide future research. First, how much of an effect do the distinguishing features defining the subtypes have on mayoral performance? Second, what happens to values such as trust among city officials when the mayor chooses to act in ways that are not compatible with the type of leadership defined by the city's form of government? Third, how much of an effect do other formal institutional features, such as salary and the electoral system, have on the mayor's performance? Fourth, does governing a large city require the executive style of mayoral leadership (and therefore use of the strong mayor–council form), or can a facilitative-style mayor (and therefore the council-manager form) successfully be used in a large city? Fifth, should a theory of mayoral leadership begin with the primacy of the formal institutional design before other contextual and proximate variables are considered?

Conclusion

The mayors in the forty largest cities in the United States increase their chances to be successful (1) if they act in ways that are compatible with the formal institutional features defining their jobs, because doing so follows the logic of appropriateness and therefore preserves trust among officials and citizens; (2) if they have the strongest version of either type of mayoral leadership; and (3) if they are supported by other formal institutional features, such as a full-time salary. It is hoped that the conceptual framework and data presented here stimulate further research on the effects that institutions have on mayoral leadership. Although formal institutional features alone do not determine mayoral performance, an institutional perspective is the foundation needed to guide the practice of politics and to develop a complete theory of mayoral leadership.

Notes

1. For three excellent reviews of the literature as well as three important theories of mayoral leadership, see Kotter, J. P., and Lawrence, P. *Mayors in Action.* New York: Wiley, 1974; Ferman, B. *Governing the Ungovernable City.* Philadelphia: Temple University Press, 1985; and Svara, J. H. *Official Leadership in the City.* New York: Oxford University Press, 1990.

2. March, J. G., and Olsen, J. P. *Rediscovering Institutions.* New York: Free Press, 1989.

3. Svara (1990).

4. March and Olsen (1989), p. 18.

5. March and Olsen (1989), p. 22.

6. March and Olsen (1989), p. 22.

7. March and Olsen (1989), p. 23.

8. March and Olsen (1989).

9. March and Olsen (1989).

10. March and Olsen (1989), p. 38.

11. Svara, J. H. "Mayoral Leadership in Council-Manager Cities: Preconditions Versus Preconceptions." *Journal of Politics,* 1987, *49,* 207–227; Svara (1990).

12. Svara (1990), p. 87.

13. Svara (1990), p. 26.

14. Svara (1990), p. 27.

15. Svara, J. H., and Associates. *Facilitative Leadership in Local Government.* San Francisco: Jossey-Bass, 1994, p. 225.

16. Svara (1990), p. 87.

17. The data on mayoral powers and other formal features in the forty largest cities (1990 population) in the United States were secured from three sources: (1) charters and statutes, (2) interviews with city officials, and (3) a follow-up letter and survey asking each mayor to verify the accuracy of the information. The data are accurate as of 1998.

18. The seventh edition of the Model City Charter offers several recommendations for designing the council-manager form of government, along with a commentary explaining the reasoning supporting each one. See National Civic League. *Model City Charter.* Denver:

National Civic League Press, 1989. Numerous academics, elected officials, and professional managers worked on the seventh edition. I use the Model City Charter as one of the sources to guide my interpretation of the importance of (1) the mayor delivering a state-of-the-city speech; (2) the mayor's power to appoint citizens to boards, commissions, and authorities; (3) the mayor's power to vote as a member of the council (so no veto power); and (4) direct election of the mayor.

19. The commentary supporting the Model City Charter also suggests that (1) a mayor should be a part-time official and (2) should not have the power to appoint assistants. Any staff support needed by a mayor should be provided by the city manager, because creating an "independent staff could lead to the mayor's encroachment on the executive responsibilities of the manager." See National Civic League (1989), p. 26.

20. See Banfield, E., and Wilson, J. Q. *City Politics.* New York: Random House, 1963, pp. 151–167. See also Bledsoe, T. *Careers in City Politics.* Pittsburgh: University of Pittsburgh Press, 1993.

21. Although the National Civic League endorsed the council-manager form in the seventh edition of the Model City Charter, it also "recognized that some cities, if properly organized, can strengthen their operations with the strong mayor and council form." See National Civic League (1989), p. 77. If a strong mayor–council form is preferred, then the National Civic League endorses allowing mayors to appoint department heads without council approval in order to prevent "provincialism and political pressures" from influencing the council in such a way as to undermine the mayor's effort to recruit personnel from other cities on the basis of professional competence. It also rejects using boards and commissions to appoint department heads, because this "dilutes" the mayor's authority and prevents him or her from acting as a "genuinely responsible executive." This argument along with other sources—including Pressman, J. L. "Preconditions for Mayoral Leadership," *American Political Science Review* 66 (June 1972): 511-524; Ferman (1985); and Svara (1990)—support my interpretation of how these two features can influence mayoral leadership.

22. See King, J. "Prop. E Would Rewrite S. F. Charter: Revision Gives More Power to Mayor, Supervisors." *San Francisco Chronicle,* Nov. 1, 1995. See also McCormick, E. "Proposition Results Seen as Call for Reform, Efficiency." *San Francisco Examiner,* Nov. 8, 1995.

23. Protasel, G. J. "Leadership in Council-Manager Cities: The Institutional Implications." In H. G. Frederickson (ed.), *Ideal and Practice in Council-Manager Government.* Washington, D.C.: International City/County Management Association, 1995.

24. Sparrow, G. W. "The Emerging Chief Executive 1971–1991: A San Diego Update." In Svara and Associates (1994).

25. Blodgett, T., and Crowley, J. C. "The Position of the Mayor in Large Council-Manager Cities." *National Civic Review,* July–Aug. 1990, *79,* 332–336.

26. Reed, S. R. "Dallas Dilemma: Headstrong Bartlett Stuck in City's Weak Mayor System." *Houston Chronicle,* July 11, 1993.

27. Bonilla, H. "Close to Home: A City Manager for the District." *Washington Post,* July 16, 1995.

28. DelVecchio, R. "Uneven Voter Turnout Sank Oakland's Strong-Mayor Proposal." *San Francisco Chronicle,* Nov. 12, 1996.

29. Pressman (1972).

30. DelVecchio, R. "The Oracle of Oakland: Jerry Brown's Style Is Less Tyrannical than Visionary." *San Francisco Chronicle,* Nov. 5, 1998.

Craig M. Wheeland is associate professor of political science at Villanova University.

Assessing the CAO Position
in a Strong-Mayor Government

Kimberly L. Nelson

Cities with elected executives require professional guidance in policy choices and professionally run government operations. A long-standing approach to meeting these needs—appointment of a chief administrative officer (CAO)—is still relevant for organizing urban government. This article examines whether and how the largest cities in the United States have incorporated this feature in their governmental structure and assesses the level of professionalism among appointed senior executives in mayor-council governments. By comparing CAOs with city managers in comparable cities, it is possible to draw conclusions about the relative professionalism and authority of CAOs in major U.S. cities.

To date, most research regarding cities operating under the mayor-council form has focused on the role of the mayor. There is no systematic information about the position of CAO.[1] Furthermore, there is wide variation in this and other features of mayor-council government. Unlike council-manager cities, which commonly follow an established plan laid out in the Model City Charter, mayor-council cities do not necessarily have a centrally appointed administrative position and differ in how they structure it.

There are two major options for cities with a CAO, and there are two approaches used in cities without a CAO. In some cities with a CAO, the roles and responsibilities of the position are formally defined in the city charter. In other cities, one person may be designated to fulfill the administrative functions, but the basis for the position is not established in the charter or city ordinance. Presumably, the position was created at the discretion of a particular mayor, although it may now be "institutionalized" and supported by experience. Cities without a single CAO are administered directly by the mayor, with several assistants or deputy mayors dividing the supervisory responsibilities or with no administrators other than department heads.

The fluid nature of the CAO position makes it difficult to establish a precise count of the number of cities that have a position with this or an equivalent title. One report suggests that 39 percent of mayor-council cities over fifty thousand in population have a city administrator.[2] It is difficult to classify mayor-council cities according to the existence and status of a CAO without carefully examining their charters and organizational charts.

The first part of this article reviews the public administration literature on the CAO. As there is little systematic knowledge about the distribution or characteristics of CAOs, there are numerous interpretations of the nature of the position. This discussion begins with Wallace Sayre's conception of the general manager plan and then addresses accountability, roles and responsibilities, and presumptions about the CAO's level of professionalism. In the second part of this article, a profile of the CAOs in the mayor-council cities among the forty largest in the United States is presented, using the same cities that Wheeland examines in his contribution to this issue. Biographies and job descriptions were compiled and analyzed for the person holding the top administrative job in the twenty-six cities that use the mayor-council form; they are compared to those of the city managers found in the other large cities. This information, along with city charters and ordinances, was used to profile the education, experience, authority, and job responsibilities of each CAO.

Conceptualizing the CAO Position:
The General Manager Plan

Writing in 1954, Sayre first articulated the concept of a strong mayor form of municipal government with an appointed CAO.[3] He argued that large cities were turning to the mayor-with-general-manager plan and away from the council-manager plan, for several reasons. First, the mayor had become an important asset to the cities as the "center of energy and public leadership and the focus of responsibility for policy and performance."[4] Second, the general manager plan added professionalism to the managerial system while still preserving the separation of powers familiar to citizens. Sayre contended that although the strong mayor would be a permanent fixture in American city government, the mayor would not be able to manage the city alone because of the "complex administrative establishments, which require strengthened central managerial leadership, direction, and coordination."[5]

The best solution, according to Sayre, was a professional manager appointed by and working alongside the mayor but at the mayor's discretion. Sayre did not propose a standardized design. Instead, he observed that the approach has evolved and been customized by each city that chose to adopt it. Indeed, Sayre viewed organizational elasticity as one of the benefits of the plan, since it increased responsiveness to local needs, preferences, and changes.[6] Outlining the major differences in five cities that used some type of general manager, Sayre reported that title, appointment, term, removal, and powers of the manager differed greatly among mayor-council cities. More recently, the academic literature on the subject has focused on accountability, roles and responsibilities, and professional experience and educational attainment relative to city managers.

Accountability of the CAO

Accountability is a basic issue in designing a CAO position. A variety of informal factors affect the relationships among mayor, CAO, and council, among them the personality and the electoral strength of the mayor, the presence of an "extraconstitutional" key adviser to the mayor who may be inserted between the mayor and the CAO, and the degree of cohesion of the council. These are certainly important, but formal factors are the focus here, particularly variations in provision for appointment and removal, that is, who hires and fires the chief administrator. These have important implications for how the CAO defines the line and scope of accountability.

There are two schools of thought regarding whether the CAO should be accountable solely to the mayor or be accountable to both the mayor and the council. The 1989 Model City Charter recommends that the CAO should serve the mayor and be appointed and removed by the mayor alone.[7] In a strong-mayor government, the charter endorses undiluted mayoral power. To this end, the charter makes no provision for specifying the CAO's authority. Instead, "the working relationship of the administrator and the mayor may well be compared to that of the executive officer of a naval vessel and his commanding officer. The mayor should be solely responsible for the appointment and removal of the administrator without any requirement of approval by the council."[8] A CAO appointed under this type of system is strictly accountable to the mayor.

Bill Hansell, executive director of the International City/County Management Association, takes a different stance. A strong advocate of the council-manager form, Hansell suggests a version of the strong-mayor form that he terms "mayor (separation of powers)-council-manager" for cities that face a great deal of conflict among elected representatives.[9] Under this form of government, the mayor acts as chief executive and nominates a manager or administrative officer whom the council must approve. Hansell's intent is to make the manager responsive to both the mayor and the council, since both are involved in the hiring decision. The manager is removable only by a majority vote of the council, and responsibilities revolve around service delivery. Hogan's research demonstrates that a close relationship exists between the mayor and CAO.[10] He found that the closer the relationship between the mayor and CAO and the greater the mayor's power, the lower the level of professionalism, authority, and scope of activity of the CAO.[11]

Data on accountability seem to support the connection between accountability and authority in the hiring decision.[12] Drawing on 1997 survey data, Svara reports that a majority of CAOs feel equally responsive to the council and mayor when the mayor must seek council approval for his hiring.[13] Conversely, most administrators believe they act as agents of the mayor when there is no council approval needed for the mayor's decision.

Roles and Responsibilities of the CAO

The responsibilities and duties of the CAO in a mayor-council city have not been clearly defined in the literature. Generally, the formal status of the CAO falls into one of two categories, as I have suggested earlier in discussing accountability. First, the CAO has formally assigned functions similar to those of a city manager in a council-manager city; or else the CAO acts as an assistant to the mayor whose responsibilities are defined by the mayor. In contrast, an administrative structure that splits the responsibilities among multiple assistants leaves the coordination and integration in the hands of the mayor, thereby increasing mayoral powers and decreasing the responsibilities of the CAO.

Because of the dearth of information regarding the specific functions of this position, it was necessary to draw from the structural provisions contained in the city charter and ordinances to determine the formal responsibilities of the chief administrator. Findings from these sources establish three tiers of formal provision. The first is basic acknowledgment or formal establishment of the CAO position in the charter. Other cities take this one step further by requiring a minimum level of education and experience in addition to recognizing the position. Finally, a minority of cities have a charter provision mandating specific duties of the administrator. Presumably, provisions such as these give the CAO greater institutional stability and autonomy.

Professionalism of the CAO

The primary argument criticizing the general manager form of government is that the CAO can be hired merely for his or her political connections to the mayor. When considering the background and qualifications of the CAO, there exists a common preconception that the CAO has a lower level of professionalism than the city manager. Terrell Blodgett argues that professional management is impossible in a city where the CAO is appointed by and accountable to the mayor exclusively.[14] He also points out that administrators in a mayor-council city are likely to have shorter tenure and less likely to have prior management experience. The appendix of the 1989 Model City Charter states that there is "no feasible way to discourage the tendency to appoint persons qualified politically rather than professionally."[15]

Since in many large cities the mayor does handle appointment of the CAO, the potential for hiring on the basis of political considerations certainly exists. However, when faced with the responsibility of managing the executive department of a large city, the mayor must consider the quality of management skills in achieving a highly functioning government. The quality of governmental performance has political implications for the mayor. When confronting the choice of whether to hire a friend or ally versus an experienced, professional manager, it is not appropriate to assume that every mayor will make the same decision about which choice is preferable.

A review of the literature suggests that although opinions about the CAO in a strong-mayor government are widespread, there has only been a limited amount of research. Hogan completed the last comprehensive study in 1976.[16] Cities have changed dramatically in the last several decades, as have their governments. This article seeks to fill in some of the gaps in the literature. This profile of government structure and CAO characteristics for the twenty-six largest (by population) mayor-council cities was created by examining biographies, charters, and ordinances. Developing a better picture of current strong-mayor government highlights needs for future research.

Investigating the CAO Position: Methodology

To address the questions I have just raised, this study used the same data set on the forty largest cities in the United States analyzed by Craig Wheeland in his article in this issue.[17] For a comparison of education and experience, information about the city managers in the thirteen council-manager cities among the forty largest was collected as well.[18]

The bulk of the research was accomplished by searching the Websites of each city. Charters and ordinances, position titles of the chief administrator, as well as job responsibilities and biographies of the administrators were sought. Follow-up phone calls were then made to request missing information directly from the city government. In some cases, newspaper archives were searched to obtain incomplete biographical information.

Organizational Placement and Status of CAO

It is reasonable to expect that variations in the formality of the position, the number of central administrators, and the method of appointment could affect the scope of responsibilities and the kind of person appointed as CAO. On the basis of an examination of the practices in twenty-six of the largest cities that use the mayor-council form of government, four categories were created (see Table 1). Answering three questions determined placement of a city in one of the four categories:

1. Does the city charter (or ordinance) recognize the chief administrative position?
2. Is there a single official in the coordinating position of CAO, or are there several key assistants, one of whom is a CAO or equivalent?
3. Is appointment of the CAO approved by the council, or does the mayor have freedom to select whomever he or she wants for the position?

The arrangements approximate a scale from high formality and broad accountability to the low formality, narrow accountability, and ambiguous status entailed by the case of having several administrators. The first two

Table 1. Status of CAO in Leading Cities with Mayor-Council Form of Government

Category 1 *Single Person;* *Council Approves;* *Formal Recognition*	Category 2 *Single Person;* *Mayor Appoints;* *Formal Recognition*	Category 3 *Single Person;* *Informal*	Category 4 *Multiple Persons*
El Paso	Houston	New York	Indianapolis
Albuquerque	New Orleans	Boston	Los Angeles
Atlanta	Washington, D.C.	Baltimore	Milwaukee
Memphis	Philadelphia	Nashville	Cleveland
Oakland	Jacksonville	Seattle	St. Louis
San Francisco		Pittsburgh	
		Chicago	
		Columbus	
		Detroit	
		Denver	
6 cities	5 cities	10 cities	5 cities

Note: It has not been verified whether the CAO position is recognized in the charter.

arrangements in the table are the most formal of the four. Cities in these categories have a single administrative manager whose position is recognized in the city's charter or ordinances.

In the first category, the mayor appoints the CAO but the council must approve the appointment. In cities classified under the second arrangement, the mayor's appointment of a CAO does not have to be approved by the council. Forty-two percent of the cities are in the first two categories. Of these eleven cities, five have administrators who are appointed by the mayor with no council approval required. Of the six cities that require council approval for appointment of an administrator, four also require that the hiring must be solely on the basis of professional qualifications. New Orleans is the only city that does not require council approval for appointment but does have a qualification statement. San Francisco is the only city in this classification that specifies the term of the CAO; it is set at five years.

Although the position of the administrators in the first two categories is formally recognized, the extent of their power may be tempered by their relationship with the mayor and the mayor's relationship with council. For example, the *Philadelphia Inquirer* reported that during the term of the city's former mayor, power was consolidated in the mayor's office, with the mayor's chief of staff holding the greatest amount of power despite the CAO's formal authority.[19]

Ten (38 percent) of the largest mayor-council cities fall in the third category. Under this arrangement, a single person usually fulfills most, if not all, of the administrative responsibilities but does so informally, at the discretion of the mayor. The city charter does not recognize the administrative position in this category. In some cases, such as Baltimore, the position was created or reinstated by the current administration.

The fourth administrative arrangement is also one of the least common, with five of the cities fitting this category. Although a general administrator may be recognized in the charter, other department heads administer one or more of the key administrative functions (budget, personnel, or operations). In Los Angeles, the city charter was recently revised. A significant change was replacement of the CAO position by a director of the Department of Operations and Research Services. This new department is responsible for budget functions only. Milwaukee has a similar arrangement with their Department of Administration. In addition to budget functions, the director of the Office of Administration also oversees intergovernmental relations, purchasing, information resources, and several programs such as community development block grants. In Indianapolis, the chief deputy mayor controls human resources and many of the operations departments but does not have control over the budget or other financial matters.

Two general characteristics across the categories should be noted. First, four-fifths of these large cities have a CAO—a proportion far higher than for mayor-council cities overall. Second, in three-quarters of the twenty-one cities with a CAO, the official is appointed by the mayor alone (categories two and three), compared to only 11 percent in all mayor-council cities with an administrator.[20]

Table 2 presents the titles of the top administrative officers and the responsibilities assigned to them in the twenty-six cities.[21] The cities are grouped according to the four categories defined earlier. The titles vary considerably, with *CAO, deputy mayor,* and *chief of staff* being the most common. The power to appoint and remove department heads is most significant and the most common distinction between council-manager and mayor-council cities. Three of the twenty-six cities grant the top administrator that power: New Orleans, Oakland, and San Francisco. In each, the CAO position is recognized in the city charter. Philadelphia also gives the managing director the power to appoint department heads but limits appointment to those departments that provide municipal services.[22]

Defining whether a CAO serves as the mayor's liaison is rather difficult. In most cases, the CAO does so informally, owing to the nature of the position. Since the CAO handles day-to-day operations of the city and reports to the mayor, he or she does serve as liaison to the mayor. In Table 2, the cities for which it is indicated that the CAO serves as the mayor's liaison have made some type of formal recognition of that responsibility, in either the charter or the job description.

Most cities grant the CAO authority over the personnel, budget, and operations departments. Philadelphia is the only city in the first two categories that does not grant the top administrative officer responsibility for the

Table 2. CAO Powers

	Title	Appoints Department Heads	Mayor's Liaison	Personnel	Budget	Operations
Category 1						
Albuquerque	CAO			X	X	X
Atlanta	Chief operating officer		X	X	X	X
El Paso	CAO	Duties delegated by mayor				
Memphis	CAO		X	X	X	X
Oakland	City manager	X		X	X	X
San Francisco	City administrator	X		X	X	X
Category 2						
Houston	CAO			X	X	X
Jacksonville	CAO			X	X	X
New Orleans	CAO	X	X	X	X	X
Philadelphia	Managing director	X		X		X
Washington, D.C.	Deputy mayor for operations and city administrator			X	X	X

Category 3

Baltimore	First deputy mayor		X	X	X
Boston	Chief operating officer		X	X	X
Chicago	Chief of staff		X	X	X
Columbus	Chief of staff		X	X	X
Denver	Chief of staff		X		
Detroit	Deputy mayor, CAO		X	X	X
Nashville	Deputy mayor		X	X	X
New York	Deputy mayor for operations		X	X	X
Pittsburgh	Deputy mayor for government operations		X		X
Seattle	Chief of staff		X	X	X

Category 4

Indianapolis	Chief deputy mayor and chief of staff	n/a	X	X	some
Los Angeles	Director of OARS			X	
Milwaukee	Director, department of administration			X	X
Cleveland	Departments administered independently	n/a	n/a	n/a	n/a
St. Louis	Executive director of operations		X	X	most

budget (the managing director, the top administrative position in Philadelphia, is primarily responsible for operations). Most of the cities in the third category also grant all three responsibilities to the top administrative officer. Denver's chief of staff serves as the mayor's liaison to all of the city departments but has no formal authority. Pittsburgh's deputy mayor for government operations has no input in the budget functions but handles personnel and operations.

Cities in the third category divide the responsibilities between several deputy mayors or department heads. Indianapolis assigns the chief deputy mayor responsibility over human resources and some operating departments, and as the mayor's liaison this position has informal authority over other departments. However, the top administrator has no input on the budget and shares authority over the operating departments with other deputy mayors. In Los Angeles, the director of the office of administrative research handles only the budget function. Milwaukee's director of the department of administration oversees the budget and most operations but not personnel.

Professional Background of CAO

It is commonly alleged that the CAO in a mayor-council city has a lower level of professionalism than the city-manager counterpart. This presumption was tested by examining the education levels and experience in city government of top administrators in mayor-council versus council-manager cities.[23] As Table 3 illustrates, sixty-five percent of CAOs in this study hold a degree above the undergraduate level. Of the twenty CAOs from the first two categories, ten have a master's degree, five of which are in public administration or political science. Three cities (Atlanta, Chicago, and Washington, D.C.) have administrators with law degrees. All of the cities in category one have administrators with a master's degree or higher. In category two, Jacksonville and Philadelphia are the only cities with administrators who do not hold a degree above the bachelor's level. There is much less consistency in the third category, where approximately 50 percent of administrators hold a master's or law degree.

Analysis of the employment experience of the CAOs shows a great deal of variation in their background. Contrary to a view of the CAO as an appointee with only political credentials, the majority of CAOs (58 percent) have prior experience at the local level. However, this finding does not necessarily indicate professional experience, since local government experience includes prior appointment to another position that may have occurred solely for political reasons. Only Boston's chief operating officer has no government experience at the federal, state, or local level. It is noteworthy that only four administrators (15 percent) worked for political parties or on the mayor's campaign.

Table 3. Experience and Education of CAO Versus City Manager

Category	Graduate Education				Experience					Political Parties and Campaigns
	M.P.A.	J.D.	M.B.A.	Other	Local Government	State Government	Federal Government	Nonprofit	Business	
(1) Individual, council approval, formal recognition	n = 1, 20 percent	n = 1, 20 percent	n = 0	n = 3, 60 percent	n = 4, 80 percent	n = 2, 40 percent	n = 2, 40 percent	n = 0	n = 1, 20 percent	n = 0
(2) Single person, no council approval, formal recognition	n = 2, 40 percent	n = 1, 20 percent	n = 0	n = 0	n = 4, 80 percent	n = 0	n = 1, 20 percent	n = 0	n = 4, 80 percent	n = 1, 20 percent
(3) Single person, informal	n = 2, 20 percent	n = 1, 10 percent	n = 1, 10 percent	n = 1, 10 percent	n = 6, 60 percent	n = 2, 20 percent	n = 2, 20 percent	n = 2, 20 percent	n = 4, 40 percent	n = 2, 20 percent
Total CAO governments (n = 20)	n = 5, 25 percent	n = 3, 15 percent	n = 1, 5 percent	n = 4, 20 percent	n = 14, 70 percent	n = 4, 20 percent	n = 5, 25 percent	n = 2, 10 percent	n = 9, 45 percent	n = 3, 15 percent
City manager governments (n = 13)	n = 8, 62 percent	n = 0	n = 1, 8 percent	n = 4, 31 percent*	n = 13, 100 percent	n = 1, 8 percent	n = 2, 15 percent	n = 0	n = 2, 15 percent	n = 0

*These four managers have degrees in political science, urban planning, or a similar area.

Professional Background of City Manager in Council-Manager City

For comparison purposes, the thirteen largest American cities using the council-manager form of government were also examined. Only one city manager lacked a postbaccalaureate degree. Additionally, all but one manager holds a degree in public administration, planning, political science, or urban studies. The city manager in Phoenix holds a master's in business. Every city manager had previous local government experience. Managers in San Antonio and San Jose also worked in the private sector. The Austin and Long Beach managers had previous experience at the state or federal government level. A majority of the city managers have worked in other cities, as opposed to being promoted from within the organization. Compared to administrators in mayor-council government, the education and experience levels of a city manager are much more consistent.

Summary and Conclusion

The largest mayor-council cities typically have a CAO, although almost one in five do not have a single person who provides administrative assistance to the mayor and council. The position is grounded in the charter in eleven of the cities that have a single CAO. When there is a CAO, the official usually has responsibility for personnel, budget, and operations, but it is rare for the CAO to have the authority to appoint department heads. The contention that mayor-council government is unlikely to have professional executives to run the administration of the city appears to be unfounded in many cases. Although the positions have clear differences, city managers and CAOs are not widely divergent in terms of professionalism, experience, and degree of administrative authority. Although the CAOs tend to score lower than city managers on the key criteria of local government professionalism—education and prior municipal management experience—the majority of large mayor-council cities have hired administrators with advanced degrees and prior experience in local government similar to those of the average manager.

In only four of the cities studied (Atlanta, Philadelphia, Detroit, and Indianapolis) does it appear that the current mayor has made the choice of administrator primarily on partisan or electoral grounds. On the other hand, some of the administrators, such as the city manager of Oakland, previously administered a council-manager form of government. The record of Albuquerque's CAO—whose appointment is approved by the council—also belies the assertion that an administrator in a mayor-council government is merely an agent of the mayor; there, Lawrence Rael has served as CAO or deputy CAO through three separate mayoral administrations.

Another case that challenges the stereotype is Nashville. The mayor of Nashville is a Democrat and has the authority to appoint the CAO, but his deputy mayor is a dedicated Republican who served in the Bush administration and as campaign chairman for several Republican campaigns.[24] Charter provisions in five cities requiring a minimum level of experience and education for the chief administrator also indicate a move toward greater professionalism in cities using the mayor-council form of government.

Cities organized under the mayor-council form decide whether to create a central administrative position and how to arrange their administrative organization. Cities have made a variety of choices, as is demonstrated by the enormous variation among the twenty-six largest mayor-council cities. Although the model charter does have a section of recommendations for a mayor-council city, it has not been used consistently. Instead, these cities have chosen to create new arrangements or to blend elements of the mayor-council and council-manager forms of government. The data from this research show a trend in the large mayor-council cities toward fusion in practice, if not in formal provision, of the professional aspects of a council-manager government with a strong mayor as chief executive. These new governmental designs address the issue of professionalism in local government, although they lead to questions of accountability, responsiveness, and maintenance of adequate authority.

If the mayor, with council approval, appoints the administrator, that person is likely to feel accountable to both parties. This situation could be problematic if policy conflict arises. Cities that give the CAO specific powers in the charter have institutionalized the position, potentially leading to CAO autonomy and lack of accountability. Cities in which control over various administrative functions is divided also face potential problems. A multiassistant approach could lead to a lower level of responsiveness and coordination in service delivery. The mayor, whose time is often limited, may find it cumbersome to oversee multiple departments personally.

Some important questions remain to be answered. How closely does the mayor follow the advice of the CAO? Are there political aides to the mayor who can override the CAO? What are the effects of other informal factors? Finally, what are the characteristics of the CAO position in the great number of cities that are smaller than those studied here? Additional research is needed to answer these questions and to improve our understanding of how well the new hybridized government forms are working.

Notes

1. The only empirical study of CAOs was by Hogan in 1976. Hogan, J. B. *The Chief Administrative Officer: An Alternative to Council-Manager Government.* Tucson: University of Arizona Press, 1976.

2. Svara, J. H. "U.S. City Managers and Administrators in a Global Perspective." *Municipal Yearbook.* Washington, D.C.: International City/County Management Association, 1999.

3. Sayre, W. S. "The General Manager Idea for Large Cities." *Public Administration Review,* 1954, *14*, 253–258.

4. Sayre (1954), p. 254.

5. Sayre (1954), p. 257.

6. Sayre (1954).

7. National Civic League. *Model City Charter.* (7th ed.) New York: National Civic League, 1989.

8. National Civic League (1989), p. 79.

9. Hansell, B. "Reforming the Reform, Part 2." *Public Management,* 1999, *81,* 27–28.

10. Hogan, J. B. *The Chief Administrative Officer.* Tucson: University of Arizona Press, 1976.

11. Hogan (1976).

12. Svara, J. H. "Do We Still Need Model Charters?" *National Civic Review,* 2001, *90*(1), 19–33.

13. Svara (2001).

14. Blodgett, T. "Beware the Lure of the 'Strong' Mayor." *Public Management,* 1994, *76,* 6–11.

15. National Civic League (1989), p. 79.

16. Hogan (1976).

17. Wheeland, C. *An Institutionalist Perspective on Mayoral Leadership: Linking Leadership Style to Formal Structure.* Villanova, Pa.: Villanova University, 2001.

18. Portland, which is in the top forty, was excluded because it uses the commission form of government.

19. Burton, C. "Street Set to Fill Key Spot Today." *Philadelphia Inquirer,* Jan. 7, 2000, p. B1.

20. Svara, J. H. (2001).

21. El Paso's CAO is currently on leave. Since the mayor assigns the duties and the position is vacant, no attempt was made to anticipate the responsibilities of a future CAO.

22. Philadelphia has a unique annotation in its charter justifying the position of managing director and describing the responsibilities of the position. The charter states that the mayor cannot supervise all departments closely; therefore the "charter attacks this problem by creating the office of managing director."

23. Since El Paso's position is vacant, there is no biographical information. Additionally, there are no data for Cleveland or Milwaukee because multiple persons fulfill administrative duties.

24. Paine, A. "Purcell Appoints Stand-In; Chief of Staff Phillips Now Deputy Mayor." *Tennessean,* Sept. 26, 2001. Online edition, downloaded Dec. 18, 2001.

Kimberly L. Nelson is a Ph.D. student in public administration at North Carolina State University.

Municipal Charters

Lawrence F. Keller

The municipal charter is a neglected area of study. Few understand its purposes, and many approach it in a highly legalistic fashion. The lack of understanding is a result of several factors, many of which have to do with how public administration and politics are studied in this country. The field of public administration in the United States focuses largely on public management in the context of the national bureaucracy. Urban political dynamics tend to be analyzed as a contest among partisan actors who can overwhelm existing structures and formal processes as they pursue personal reward with scant regard for a broader public interest. Furthermore, a growing number of urban observers focus on community projects and public participation and underestimate the importance of structures and processes, finding in the broad participation of citizens the true meaning of urban politics. Finally, attorneys are trained clinically and thus approach municipal law from a black-letter perspective. They generally do not think in terms of the spirit of municipal laws as an expression of the nature of a given community.

A better understanding of municipal charters can perhaps be reached by reconsidering the nature of municipalities more deeply. A municipality is an empowered government directly controlled by its citizens. Citizens not only create municipalities but can also terminate them. No other government is so completely susceptible to the collective wishes of its citizens. Most Americans live in a municipality, and since it is governed according to its charter, charters are of major significance for the quality of public life for most Americans.

This article develops a relatively complete perspective on municipalities that highlights the crucial role of charters in the political life of this country. After a brief sketch of the historical origins of the municipality as a form of government, a concept of the municipality as an empowered polity that maximizes the ability of citizens to participate in public life is developed. From this perspective, the municipal charter can be seen as the blueprint for effective participation and just governance.

Roman Origins of the Municipality

Rome developed several political innovations that are the historical cornerstone of modern society and its governance. For example, Roman citizenship was extended to those with no Roman blood. The Bible records St. Paul halting the judicial process in Judaea by proclaiming to a Roman court his rights as a Roman citizen. Nowhere was innovation more necessary than in governing the highly diverse cities that Rome conquered.

Roman leaders realized that local policies could vary without having that affect their ultimate control over the empire. They conceived of the city as a separate legal entity, called a municipality, and granted it the authority to direct its own local affairs. The word *municipal* refers to the internal affairs of a governmental entity. Thus Rome controlled the external affairs of the empire, and cities were able to direct affairs within their own boundaries. These Roman municipalities were the origin of the municipal corporation in American law.

The Making of Modern America

From approximately 1880 to 1920, population growth in American municipalities exploded. The United States metamorphosed from an agrarian nation to a country dominated by large cities. New York City, formed during this time by the merger of the largest and third largest American cities, grew by a million people each decade from 1880 to 1920. Cleveland, Ohio, went from a city of 50,000 in 1880 to a metropolis of 720,000 by 1920. Spurred by industrial development based on abundant natural resources, this population growth was centered almost entirely in the northeastern and midwestern sections of the country. By 1920, the United States was the major industrial power of the world, with several cities of over a million people.

Rapid urbanization and industrialization created problems beyond the capacity of the political system. Reformers of every stripe and persuasion arose, offering solutions to burgeoning problems. Some of these reformers focused on governance of the rapidly growing cities. The initial response to the political dynamics of growth had been government by a patronage machine controlled by a political party. This system often placed considerable public power in the hands of nonpublic officials (typically the county chair of the dominant party). Although the political machine helped to integrate immigrants into American life, this style of one-party rule rarely afforded solutions to urban problems, which helped create an opening for state officials to interfere with municipal politics.

This involvement from state officials was typically partisan in motivation. State legislative control over agencies and policies at the local level meant that a political party in control of the state government could use power to direct patronage and other policies at the municipal level. This prompted reformers to propose controls on the ability of state government to intervene in municipal affairs. They fought for "home rule," the ability of a city to develop its own government without interference from state government.

Some states implemented home rule by statute. Others secured home rule for their municipalities by amending their constitution. Ohio, for example, added Article XVIII to the state constitution in 1912. The article secured home rule in the broadest terms: "Municipalities shall have authority to exercise all powers of local self-government and to adopt and enforce within their limits such local police, sanitary and other similar regulations, as are not in conflict with general laws." In addition, the article granted all municipalities the ability to design their own government: "Any municipality may frame and adopt or amend a charter for its government and may . . . exercise thereunder all powers of local self-government." This broad grant of home rule in municipal government, and similar provisions in many other states, elevated the importance of the charter. It became in essence a constitution—the governing document, specifying how the municipality was to be constituted as a political community.

Charters and the Law

Local government in the United States is a creature of state government. Even though most states permit some form of home rule, its extent depends upon the nature and interpretation of state law. The courts view constitutional and nonconstitutional entities quite differently and often permit exercises of authority by a constitutional entity (federal government, state government) if such measures are not expressly prohibited by the constitution. In contrast, for a nonconstitutional entity (such as a city under a home rule system) courts may prohibit a particular exercise of authority unless it is explicitly granted. This restriction emphasizes the importance of a well-crafted charter. A well-designed city charter is of great help in dealing with court interpretation by providing clear and explicit language for critical governance functions.

The municipality is a corporation. As such, it must have a charter that clearly declares objectives, grants authority, and establishes processes for obtaining corporate objectives. This underscores the legal fact that a charter is not a constitution and needs more specificity to ensure its adherence to constitutional requirements. The breadth and reach of a charter depends not only upon its content but also on the legal context of state law, as we have noted. If a state has enacted a constitutionally based, encompassing system of home rule, as Ohio did with Article XVIII of its constitution, a charter can take on many characteristics of a constitution.

The expansion of rights and liberties under the national constitution has limited certain of the powers of the municipality. For example, the city of Cincinnati passed an ordinance declaring particular sections of the city to be drug zones, and it gave police the authority to examine people entering such zones or exclude them from doing so. The court struck down this exercise of the municipal police power as a violation of the federally guaranteed right of travel as well as a violation of the limits of home rule authority under the Ohio constitution.

The most important limitation on the municipality is the state law on municipal home rule. A court response to home rule authority depends first upon whether the provision of municipal home rule is constitutional or statutory. Also, court interpretation depends upon how broad the grant of home rule is. Finally, as home rule is now a century old, case law itself may be a source of limitation on municipal authority. The Model City Charter developed by the National Civic League is of great help in dealing with these limitations because it calls attention to critical issues in framing a valid charter and offers careful language to achieve general municipal objectives.

Though a charter faces legal limitations that differentiate it from a constitution, its political function is to constitute the municipality, and as such a charter is directly related to the quality of public life in the municipality. The political function is thus supremely important and demands careful conceptual analysis, as it can easily be lost in a misplaced concern with legal restriction or in approaching the charter from a technical orientation.

The Constitutive Function of the Municipal Charter Constitution

Creation of the modern nation state led to the rise of the modern city. Feudalism was eroded by the rise of cities, where citizens were free of feudal restrictions. In fact, running away to a city was a primary method of obtaining freedom from feudal obligations. In many European nations, the monarchy arose by aligning itself politically with the increasingly important cities. Thus the homes of many monarchs were transferred from remote castles selected for protection to capital cities, which often became the dominant city for the nation (London, Paris, and Berlin are just the obvious examples). The city became the abode of free men whose freedoms were typically embedded in a royal charter granted by the monarch.

Initially, charters were for the most part fairly general—such as the Magna Carta, extracted from a reluctant King John. Eventually they became more specific and encompassed such things as a grant of freedom from commercial liability to those promoting economic development. These commercial charters are the basis for the modern corporation. However, the most significant charters for the quality of public life were, and remain, municipal charters. A municipal charter granted to the city almost complete domestic control over public life. For all but foreign affairs, it was the basis for organizing public life for the city. This remains the function of the municipal charter; consequently it performs the critical political office of constituting the municipality.

The municipal charter details the authority of the city, the structure of the government, and the processes by which the government exercises authority.

State law often defines the authority of the city. However, in many cases, a city may assume all (or only part) of the authority granted by state law. A city may determine that some functions are to be performed by state agencies. For example, a city may decide to have the county or similar unit of state government plan for the municipality.

Some state laws may require a city to declare explicitly its intention to exercise specific authority. Conversely, state laws may permit a city to opt out of some authority by stating in its charter the intention to do so. An example of the latter is the ability to exempt the city from state civil service provisions. In all cases, the charter must be clear on the intent. This is not just a matter of legal nicety; it demands careful and clear writing of key provisions. Again, a model charter can be of crucial support by offering examples of provisions—and, just as importantly, the reasons for such provision. A major strength of the Model City Charter is the commentary describing the nature of the provision and the major options around important functions.

The governing structure of a municipality is obviously important. Another critical function of the Model City Charter is that it states certain preferences on structure. Government is not an organization separate from the community; it is the means by which a political community makes decisions. Conceptually, this is the meaning of the term republic, how public things (*res* means "thing" in Latin) are to be handled. Private things are left to individuals and such other institutions as the family and religious organizations. Government handles public things, the structure and processes the community has established for that purpose.

Though many conceptions of republic exist, all emphasize the accountability of government to the people. People in this sense are not just voters, or even the current generation of citizens. *People* refers to past, present, and future citizens to which the current government must be accountable. The inclusion of "to us and our posterity" in a municipal charter is not just a rhetorical flourish but recognition that accountability is cross-generational. Accountability includes concern for the future effects of policy as well as sensitivity to the traditions of the past.

Community decisions must be produced by institutions that are established through politically legitimate means—that is, the institution must be part of the formal fabric of the community. It must be based on the constitution, either specifically embodied in it or created by the processes of government established by it. Americans are uniquely a political people; our identity is not an ethnic one. An American is a person who accepts and acts out specific political values, the values that constitute the American polity. Our revolution was a political event, based on a belief that public policy and administrative implementation must reflect constitutional values. Failure to follow the values invalidates actions of government and, in fact, legitimates opposition.

Public authority, the ability to act in the name of the polity, is allocated to offices within a duly constituted institution. Participation is best conceptualized as holding office. From this perspective, a republic is democratic if public offices are open to all qualified citizens. Politically, public schools facilitate expansion of the pool of qualified citizens by teaching both the nature of government and a duty to participate. Perhaps the clearest example of participation by holding office is the jury system. No citizen may be declared a criminal by the community without the unanimous concurrence of fellow citizens. Legally, the failure to establish a jury selection process that faithfully represents the community invalidates any conviction.

Writing a Charter

Many of the historic cities that were republics or democracies traced their civic roots to a lawgiver. Solon and Hammurabi are perhaps the best known. Americans trace their roots to a founding, involving a convention of lawgivers. Conceptually, home rule empowers citizens to create a government. To discharge this power effectively, citizens need well-crafted processes and resources. This is particularly the case when home rule provisions allow a citizen-led mechanism to create a charter. In Ohio, for example, a charter commission develops a charter. The commission is a fifteen-member body elected at large in the municipality. It must write a proposed charter and submit it to the voters by the next election. They cannot discharge their duty effectively unless they are given sufficient resources.

The resources are not just financial. A charter commission requires educated members acting professionally with informed and responsive staff. Providing such staff could be a function of the public urban university. Faculty in such an institution could assist citizens in discharging their public duties by holding them to constitutional norms. Armed with a civic education, most citizens would act professionally, seeking what is best for their community.

A final ingredient in creating an effective and just charter is an agenda. The Model City Charter has performed this role well in all the charter and charter review commissions with which I have worked. The commentary in the model charter helps educate citizens on the choices they must make. It also makes clear that the preferred form of government has many advantages and thus any deviation from it requires demonstrable support. This has helped create a more aware form of council-mayor government in many cases, as citizens realize the consequences of an elected (rather than appointed) chief executive. The decision about the nature and selection of the chief executive is for the citizens to make, but they should know the consequences of how the chief executive is selected.

In sum, implementing operational home rule requires citizens to be able to design and implement effective and just governance. This requires civic knowledge, constitutional and professional norms, prudent political judgment, professional staff, and a model charter as an agenda. Such civic institutions as public schools and public urban universities are an important part of this mix.

Conclusion: Back to the Empowered Municipality

A charter is a critical public document. It organizes the government closest to the citizen and the one over which they have the most control. A home rule charter gives citizens an unparalleled opportunity for realizing a just and effective corporate political reality at the local level.

This realization is difficult in modern America; the post–World War II era of highway construction and suburb development created a metropolitan America that was quite different from the urban landscape that preceded it. As a result, states must now cope with sprawl, which is often driven by small independent municipalities that use home rule for the benefit of local politicians, parties, developers, and real estate interests. Though such private use of public authority is not new, its effects are more widespread than previously. Hopefully, the response to such problems will not negate the benefits of home rule and local control. States must approach the problem of urban sprawl with an understanding of the benefits of home rule, the centrality of urban life in American politics, and discrimination among types of municipality. This is not easy, but how well it is done may well determine the quality of public life in America.

Lawrence F. Keller is a faculty associate at the Public Administration Program in the Levin College of Urban Affairs at Cleveland State University.

Regionalism in Metropolitan Chicago: A Work in Progress

David K. Hamilton

Local governments have struggled to maintain their autonomy and simultaneously deal with the increasing interconnectedness of public issues. To provide specific regional services, special districts have been established. Governments, particularly in the suburbs, have established councils of governments (COGs) to discuss issues that transcend their individual boundaries, and in many instances they have joined together to offer a specific service to member governments.

Business leaders in many metropolitan areas, recognizing the obstacles that local political leaders encounter in addressing regional policy issues, have also played a role in developing regional governance initiatives. Business leaders in Chicago started a regional governance initiative in 1999 called Chicago Metropolis 2020. This is not the first organization in Chicago to become involved in regional issues. Indeed, many other business-funded civic organizations have been involved in studying regional issues, producing reports, and advocating regional action on specific issues for many years. Metropolis 2020 takes regionalism to a new level. Its agenda is not narrowly focused on one or two regional governance issues but on a much broader goal of a comprehensive regional governance system. This initiative is an example of new regionalism.

New regionalism involves collaboration among the public and private sectors on issues dealing with metropolitan governance. These efforts may include a decision-making process on regional issues, brokering a cooperative arrangement among governments in the region, and inducing state legislation, when necessary, to implement a regional solution. In contrast to previous approaches to regional governance, new regionalism does not involve restructuring government boundaries or altering authority relationships among local municipal governments. There is strong involvement by the private sector, which for the purposes of this article includes civic agencies that are involved in regional activity and dependent upon the private sector or private foundations for financial and leadership resources.

New regionalism is a collaborative, nonhierarchical process where each party comes to the table as a relatively equal participant in decision making.

Because all participants are peers, a commitment to consensus building and shared leadership in resolving issues is a prerequisite to the success of the endeavor. The participants invariably have their own self-interest but usually develop a group synergy that extends their scope of influence and range of expertise and creates a legitimacy that they lack on their own. Consequently, the collaborative effort is held together by the advantages each participant perceives in mutual involvement.[1] In some instances, a collaborative alliance may form to address only one issue, but the same core people may be involved in a number of single-purpose alliances. The result is an interlocking web of public and private people involved in a number of regional issues so that even a single-purpose issue receives a broad focus.

This article reviews the literature on the new regionalism activity in selected metropolitan areas to identify elements that successful initiatives have in common. This framework is then used to analyze the efforts of two regional organizations in Chicago: Chicago Metropolis 2020, the initiative begun by area business leaders; and the Metropolitan Mayors Caucus, a regional forum established in 1997. The Mayors Caucus is an informal, COG-like body that allows elected political leaders to meet, discuss, and possibly take action on issues of regional significance. These two organizations seem to have the best potential for fostering regionwide governance in the area. Information for this analysis was gathered through consulting minutes, internal reports, and publications of the two organizations and through interviews with selected political and business leaders and staff of organizations involved in the regionalism effort.[2]

Successful New Regionalism

The public and private sectors each have different roles to play in making regional governance mechanisms successful.

The Role of the Civic Sector. The private sector has been an advocate for regional reform since at least the early part of the twentieth century. In the 1960s, the private sector was particularly active in pushing consolidation of governments to reduce political fragmentation or, alternatively, in advocating metropolitan government to establish overall political control for the region. These efforts met with limited success, as there was only a handful of consolidations and no metropolitan governments were formed in the United States.[3] The private sector has largely backed away from advocating structural reform and started to work collaboratively with the public sector on solving regional governance issues.

Researchers point to the need for a thriving community-oriented civic infrastructure for any new regionalism effort to succeed. Political scientist Robert Putnam found in his research of regional government in Italy that areas with a historically strong civic infrastructure and an informed and involved electorate had more effective regional government than areas without these attributes. A civic network fosters communication and interaction among peers. The greater the communication among peers, other things being equal, the greater their ability to develop mutual trust and to cooperate and work together. Civic involvement on the basis of shared interest transcends narrow self-interest and promotes cooperative behavior for the good of the whole. A web of competing interests balances the narrow interest of one group with those of other groups. Thus, the civic infrastructure moves the discussion to a higher level that transcends government boundaries and individual self-interest.[4]

Civic organizations transcend political boundaries and are in the most advantageous position to develop and nurture a network of private, nonprofit, and government organizations to address regional governance concerns. Civic agencies can also function as a neutral third party in providing staff support and conducting research to keep issues on the public agenda. In their study of regionalism initiatives and public-private collaboration in the Silicon Valley and other areas, Henton, Melville, and Walesh indicate that the forum where government and private leaders meet is the civic sector. It is the neutral zone between government and business where issues can be discussed and relationships can be developed without political boundaries and any immediate business agenda interfering. Henton and colleagues suggest that civic entrepreneurs are the key to successful regionalism. These civic leaders have contacts in the government community who are able to bring the various stakeholders together and facilitate discussion and action on decisions.[5]

A Committee for Economic Development study identified essential ingredients for successful public-private cooperation:

- A positive civic culture rooted in a practical concern for the community as a whole that encourages citizen participation
- A realistic and commonly accepted vision of the community that takes into account strengths and weaknesses in identifying what the community can and should become
- Effective building-block civic organizations that blend the self-interest of their members with the broader interest of the community and translate that dual interest into effective action
- A network among the key groups that encourages communication among leaders of every important segment and facilitates mediation of differences among competing interests
- The inclination to nurture civic entrepreneurs—leaders whose knowledge, imagination, and energy are directed toward enterprises that benefit the community, whether in the public sector, the private sector, or both
- Continuity in policy, including the ability to adapt to changing circumstances, which minimizes uncertainty and fosters confidence in individual and group enterprise[6]

Leadership of Regional Efforts. Initiation and leadership of the new regionalism effort are more likely to come from the private sector than from politicians. Many, if not most, recent efforts to promote collaboration have been initiated and supported by the private sector. Indeed, social scientist Kathryn Foster advances the thesis that regionalism is basically a private affair with hesitant public sector participants pulled into the process. That is, private interests initiate the process, establish the agenda, fund the effort, and use their considerable influence to push for acceptance of their proposals. According to Foster, public sector leadership has a weak regional focus, whereas corporate, civic, and academic leaders are more regionally focused. They generally see their interest as regional rather than restricted by a political boundary.[7]

Research by Henton, Melville, and Walesh in the Silicon Valley and elsewhere supports Foster's assertion on the critical role of the private sector in the initiation of regionalism efforts. For example, the business leaders in Silicon Valley responded to a severe economic recession in the early 1990s, the result of defense cuts and a restructuring in high-tech manufacturing, by forming Joint Venture: Silicon Valley, a nonprofit organization to improve the regional economy. It involves more than two hundred business, government, education, and community leaders in developing and implementing plans to improve the economic and quality of life in the region.[8] In Atlanta, city and suburban business and government leaders collaborated on winning the competition for the 1996 Summer Olympics; out of necessity, they had to collaborate on hosting the Olympics. Through this collaborative effort, networks and relationships were formed that continue as the leaders address regional issues.[9]

Broad Community Involvement. Examples of successful regional governance in the United States invariably show that broad involvement is important, not just on the part of the business community but from other sectors of the community as well. In the structural reform effort in Indianapolis, the role of the League of Women Voters and the chamber of commerce was important in keeping the reform issue on the public agenda. The Greater Indianapolis Progress Committee, a bipartisan citizens group representing a spectrum of the community, was probably the most successful of numerous government-sponsored study groups. This group has been institutionalized as a valuable component of the civic community.[10]

Traditional civic agencies may not be adequate to engender broad involvement. Minneapolis and St. Paul are a case in point. The Twin Cities metropolitan area has familiar civic organizations, but the one that seems to be most successful in regionalism issues is the little-known citizens league. It is characterized by the ability to bring about the intimate and sustained involvement of a variety of interested citizens in public affairs. The league was created in 1952 as an outgrowth of years of informal discussion on public issues among civic-minded Twin Cities businesspeople. Membership is open to anyone who is willing to pay the minimal annual dues. There are about three thousand individual members and six hundred supporting firms and foundations. Each year the league studies a number of issues of interest to its members. It forms a task force for each topic, which holds meetings, invites experts, and conducts discussions until a consensus is reached. A report is then written, widely disseminated, debated, and sometimes modified by the league's board. In bringing together people from various sectors of the community, the league fosters informal networks in which people are able to work with each other as issues arise.[11]

Every region that has experienced success in bringing people together to address regional issues uses its own approach to obtain broad community involvement. In some regions, the citizens league model is used. For example, the Citizens League of Greater Cleveland, an organization with two thousand members, has been influential in pushing cooperation among governments and in fostering a regional governance culture. It issues reports and publications with a regional focus, including *Rating the Region,* a report that shows how well or poorly the Cleveland area compares against similar areas on various economic and social indicators. Other regions that have citizens leagues are Indianapolis, Charlotte, and Oklahoma City.[12] Philadelphia uses another model, with some success. The Center for Greater Philadelphia, an applied public policy unit at the University of Pennsylvania, holds annual conferences and related seminars to bring together government and corporate leaders and citizens to mobilize grassroots support for regional awareness and regional action. One of the center's successes has been facilitating development of a regional legislative agenda for state legislators.[13]

Civic Agency as a Facilitator of New Regionalism. A civic agency that desires to promote positive public policy outcomes among disparate and often conflictual groups must be perceived as neutral and not biased toward any group involved in the process. It cannot be connected with any specific government involved or any private or nonprofit enterprise that stands to gain directly from a proposed solution. In other words, the agenda should be simply to facilitate a collaborative process to reach a mutually acceptable solution on a public policy issue. The answers must emerge from the interaction of the stakeholders.[14]

Denver is an example of how a civic agency facilitated a solution to developing a new water supply for the Denver region's growing population. There was substantial contention on this issue involving the Denver Water Board, suburban water suppliers, developers, environmentalists, and west-slope interests that did not want water diverted into the Denver region. A nonprofit organization acted as a neutral facilitator to work with the interested parties to mediate a solution. Through a process of meetings, small working groups, and proposal and counterproposal, basic agreements were reached in less than half the time required in a previous effort to increase the water supply to the region. Moreover, the bitter feelings felt for years in the last experience were not evident in this effort. The factors contributing to the success of this effort include the urgency of the situation, high-level political leadership from a governor who did not try to force a solution, participant ground rules that ruled out partisanship, and broad inclusion of parties affected by the issue. In addition, there was a well-structured decision-making process operating under a consensus decision rule, an iterative step-by-step agreement process, and closed meetings to facilitate honest and open discussion that promoted development of trust between adversaries.[15]

Public Sector Involvement and Support for New Regionalism. Obviously, for business to maximize its influence in regional governance issues there must be public sector leaders who are receptive to partnering with the private sector, and they must be in a position to affect public policy. The major problem is that there is generally no political entity at the regional level with authority over the geographical area similar to a municipal government. This makes coalition building by the private sector difficult. Because there is no regional political constituency, it also makes the business sector that much more critical in initiating new regionalism. It also results in a regional agenda that invariably revolves around development issues. However, many public issues of a social nature, such as ensuring an adequate supply of affordable housing among municipalities in the region, have been agenda items for new regionalism.

In some regions, there may be a constituted legal authority with developmental authority that the private sector can interact with to influence policy. This is the situation in the Portland (Oregon) and Minneapolis regions, with their metropolitan councils. In states or metropolitan areas that have an aggressive county government with authority to provide regional services, the private sector may turn to the county political leaders to develop a partnership. Sometimes a loose coalition of local governmental leaders is formed with the private sector to develop and implement regional policies or jointly to lobby the state on regional issues of common interest. In any event, the private sector cannot be successful in the public policy arena without the support and involvement of the public sector.

To summarize this discussion, here are the elements that facilitate a successful new regionalism initiative:

- There must be an opportunity or a crisis. In the Denver region, it was the crisis of a dwindling water supply; in the Silicon Valley, it was the economic downturn in the early 1990s; in Atlanta, it was the opportunity offered by the 1996 Olympics. The opportunity or crisis does not by itself perpetuate or sustain a regionalism initiative.
- Top business leadership must initiate the effort or be actively invested in the effort after it is initiated. Business leadership must give liberally of time and resources to make the effort successful.
- An active civic sector must be in place to promote networking and communitarian concerns.
- There must be a civic agency to spearhead the effort. The civic agency should have the full support of business leadership, and the leaders of the

agency must have a good working relationship with local and state political leaders. It should have adequate staff resources, facilitate and guide the process, be action-oriented rather than a report generator, and monitor implementation of any action plan. As facilitator of the process, the agency must remain objective and not advocate a specific solution. The process cannot be perceived as being dominated by business or central city interests.

• Broad involvement from other leaders and citizens in the region is important for successful regionalism. All geographic areas and sectors of the community affected by the issues should be involved in the deliberative process that arrives at a solution.

• Appropriate political leaders from throughout the region should be actively involved in the process to facilitate government action.

New Regionalism in Chicago

Regional governance is very much a work in progress in the metropolitan Chicago area. This section examines two of the most promising developments, the Metropolitan Mayors Caucus and Chicago Metropolis 2020.

The Political Environment. The Chicago region is noted for its political fragmentation and antagonism between the central city and suburbs. With more than 940 local governments possessing taxing authority, it has the most local governments of any metropolitan area in the nation. The city has dominated the region politically as well as economically for most of its history. Strategies used by Chicago to extend its boundaries and otherwise dominate the suburbs have left many suburbs hostile and apprehensive. Until recently, there was a total lack of cooperation and unwillingness to work together on issues affecting the region. This legacy of distrust, as well as differences in political party representation and the divergent needs of the central city and suburban populations, have been difficult to bridge.

One major issue causing friction between Chicago and the suburbs is noise pollution. The municipalities around O'Hare Airport want Chicago to institute noise reduction strategies and not add additional runways. In addition, people in the suburbs blame Chicago as being the main source of crime, corruption, social decay, and physical deterioration in the metropolitan area. They feel Chicago has looked to other governments for subsidies long enough, and it needs to get its own house in order before looking to other governments for financial assistance.

Suburbanites' wariness and jealousy are not just directed at Chicago. Historically, suburban municipalities have not extensively cooperated among themselves. They have competed with each other either for economic development or to keep it out; they have squabbled over unincorporated land or road and residential development on their borders. Suburbs with an extensive tax base have not cooperated with those not so well endowed. Because of great diversity, it was unusual when suburbs could agree on a common agenda to present to the state legislature or common goals for the future of the region as a whole. There is no common theme that binds them together, except their historical distrust of Chicago.

Until recently, Chicago and its needs dominated the agenda of the state legislature. Democrats controlled the legislative body, and the Chicago legislative delegation was tightly united and responsive to the needs of Chicago. Although the suburban legislators generally were Republicans, they were not united on their own needs nor united against those of Chicago. One observer of the Chicago scene analyzes the Chicago dominance this way:

> For much of the postwar era, Chicago was able to exercise power in the state legislature by striking bargains with downstate rural Republicans and Democrats, and the suburbs were generally left out of such deals. The difficulties that suburban Republicans had in influencing legislative deal making stemmed in part from their more ideological orientation toward politics. In any event, making deals with Chicago Democrats was not good politics for suburban representatives, because these politicians had long made Chicago corruption a key rallying point. Overt anti-Chicago sentiment served Republican suburban representatives well during their campaigns and later, when building legislative coalitions.[16]

As a result of redistricting following the 1990 census, the Republicans gained control of the state legislative body in the 1994 election. The majority leaders in both legislative bodies were suburban Republicans. Within weeks of the opening of the 1995 session, the Republicans started exercising their will on the city. Nearly one hundred bills were introduced in the state legislature to limit or strip power from various city boards, districts, and offices and shift it to the state or the suburbs.[17] The legislature ignored the request by Mayor Richard Daley, Jr., for special legislation to authorize casino gambling in Chicago and instead authorized river boat gambling and approved a number of licenses for floating casinos on the Fox River, less than an hour's drive from Chicago.

The state also reacted coolly to Chicago's request for a new regional airport on the South Side and started pushing an alternative site in the far south suburbs. There was also a movement to establish a state airport authority that would operate O'Hare and the new airport in the far south suburbs, effectively removing O'Hare from Chicago's control. To thwart this movement, Chicago established a bistate airport authority with Indiana to keep O'Hare under its control.[18] Relations between the city and the state did not improve until the Democrats took control of the General Assembly and a new Republican governor was elected.

Civic Activism and Regionalism in Chicago. Chicago has a rich history of civic activism. Most of it, however, has been by Chicago-based civic agencies and directed at policy issues within the boundaries of the city. Chicago's political leaders saw no need to form a regional alliance and opposed regionalism as a potential dilution of their political power.[19] Any need for regional service delivery was handled through establishment of a special district. Because of Chicago's political dominance in the region and the state, any regional initiative had to receive Chicago's blessing and support. Indeed, regional special districts were usually established to provide resources to Chicago. For example, creation of the Regional Transportation Authority in 1974 to oversee funding of the public transit system in the region was the result of Chicago's need to obtain revenue from the entire metropolitan area to keep the Chicago Transit Authority running.[20]

For a number of years, the two major agencies involved in metropolitan issues were the Northeastern Illinois Planning Commission (NIPC), a state-established planning agency; and the Metropolitan Planning Council (MPC), a business-backed civic agency. NIPC had no authority over local governments; MPC was not a high-profile organization and was not a major interest of the business community. MPC was also viewed in the suburbs as being oriented to dealing with Chicago's problems through regional solutions. Regionalism was not a major concern to political and business leadership.

In the last few years, the image of a Chicago not interested in regional governance has changed dramatically with establishment of the Metropolitan Mayors Caucus and Chicago Metropolis 2020. In addition, a number of other civic agencies were established or reinvigorated to bring a stronger focus to regional issues. Regionalism, which for so long was either ignored or reviled, is now a major public agenda item. The shifting political fortunes of Chicago Democrats led to outreach effort toward suburban political leaders to form coalitions on issues in common. Some observers also speculate that Mayor Daley's tenure as president of the U.S. Conference of Mayors changed his view on the benefits of discussing issues in common with other mayors and made apparent the advantages of united action.

As the political climate changed, business interest in regionalism also increased. New regionalism was becoming more of a topical issue across the country; metropolitan areas such as the Twin Cities, Pittsburgh, Silicon Valley, and Portland reported some successful initiatives. At the same time, a local business civic group, the Civic Committee, was looking for a public issue around which to mobilize the business community, somewhat similar to the way the Burnham Plan had energized the business community at the beginning of the twentieth century.

Metropolitan Mayors Caucus. An outreach effort by Mayor Daley resulted in establishment of the Metropolitan Mayors Caucus in 1997. The caucus is an informal group composed of the eight COGs that cover the metropolitan area. All mayors belong through their respective COG. Each COG can bring the director of the COG and up to eight mayors to quarterly meetings. The Chicago city government provides most of the staff; schedules the meetings; and prepares the minutes, records, and reports of caucus activities. However, the caucus has recently incorporated as a 501(c)(3) organization and obtained a grant to hire an executive director and establish offices separate from Chicago city government.

The work of the caucus is conducted through task forces staffed by the COGs and Chicago. The mayors who do not regularly attend meetings can serve on a task force. (The Appendix to this article lists the task forces, their goals, and accomplishments.) With the investment of time and effort in the process on the part of the mayors and COG staff, ownership and commitment to results are promoted. Although the caucus was the result of a Chicago initiative and is kept alive by Chicago, active task force involvement of suburban mayors ensures that a regional perspective is maintained.

The caucus has avoided tackling disruptive city-suburban issues since its founding. This is changing, however, as it recently held a meeting on airport capacity, which indicates a willingness at least to talk about divisive matters. That this issue remains contentious and could disrupt the harmony of the caucus is an understatement. Another controversial issue that the caucus is considering is smart growth. The long-term effectiveness of the caucus depends on how well the city and the suburbs are able to work out differences over these and other issues that have divided them.

An advantage of the caucus is that members can participate but are not obliged to abide by a decision. Thus, it is a safe forum for discussion of sensitive regional issues. It also promotes networking between mayors and COG executives in what is becoming an institutionalized setting. Furthermore, it is a mechanism for identifying activities where joint action can be taken to produce cost savings for individual municipalities, and for organizing lobbying at the state level for policies of mutual benefit to metropolitan communities.

Chicago Metropolis 2020. Chicago Metropolis 2020 was established as a civic agency in 1999 to implement the goals of the Commercial Club.[21] Although it has its own executive council, staff, and separate funding, the imprimatur of the Commercial Club is readily visible in Metropolis 2020. The president of the club appointed the initial executive council, and club members constitute more than half of the council. Of the forty-six members of the original council appointments, twenty-six are or have been connected with the business community. They are generally the presidents (or retired presidents) of their organizations. There is a chairman, a president and chief executive officer, and a full-time executive director.

The president and chief executive officer, retired Inland Steel President George Ranney, Jr., is the driving force behind the organization. His vision of the purpose and mission permeates Metropolis 2020 and provides direction. The organization, although not envisioned as a permanent agency, has no sunset provisions. It is currently in the second year of a three-year funding commitment of more than $4 million provided largely by the MacArthur Foundation.

The professional staff is small—three professional staff members who are assigned to specific projects. In addition, there are currently four volunteers, called senior executive staff; two are current or former council members who have taken on specific projects of interest to them. They may provide their own staff or call on Metropolis 2020 staff to assist them. Senior executive staff are currently involved in workforce development, early childhood education, public safety and juvenile justice, health care, and affordable housing issues. The professional staff is working on development of a state-of-the-region report, taxes, metropolitan growth, housing, land use, and transportation issues.

The council meets quarterly to hear and approve reports, but council members have the opportunity to serve on a task force to oversee and give direction to professional staff on a specific project. People who are not council members with expertise in a specific project area are often recruited to be members of a task force. Outside experts may also be impaneled as a board of advisors for a project. In theory, the staff works under the direction of the task force until the project is completed. The task forces operate fairly independently of the council. The organization was purposely designed to be an action-oriented agency, not a planning agency or a policy think tank. It sees itself as a catalyst to complement and assist other organizations involved in the same public policy issues. It can permit additional access to political decision makers, as well as resources and focus for these issues. For public issues that it wishes to champion with no organized advocacy group, it takes the lead.

Metropolis 2020 has been both praised and criticized. It is praised for organizing the top echelon of the business community to advocate for public policy issues in a way that has not happened in recent memory. Not only is the top echelon of the business sector involved on the governing council, but respected community business and nonprofit leaders with access to the political establishment have volunteered time and effort to work on specific issues.[22] With their leadership and access into the political establishment plus the backing of the business leaders of major corporations, Metropolis 2020 is a formidable pressure group.

On the other hand, Metropolis 2020 is perceived as an elitist organization directed and tightly controlled by leaders of the business community. Business leaders hold all the leadership positions on the council. Even though it has made an effort to include nonbusiness people on its council, members not closely connected to the upper echelons of the business community are a distinct minority; the forty-six-member council has just one union leader, one religious leader, and three suburban mayors.[23]

The report that gave birth to Metropolis 2020 was controversial, and some of the recommendations have met substantial resistance from governmental leaders. One recommendation, for consolidation of two planning agencies and transfer of all transportation planning, was rejected by the three agencies involved in transportation planning, but the recommendation seems to have resulted in a better effort at coordination by the agencies. Although not backing off its commitment to implement the recommendations from the report, the group has downplayed some of the more controversial ones. It has chosen to work on less contentious objectives contained in the report and is also working on two issues that are not part of the report's numerous recommendations (public safety and juvenile justice). These are issues championed by a volunteer executive.

Metropolis 2020 has been praised for putting the concept of regionalism forcefully before community leadership. It is now a public policy topic, whereas previously it was much less visible. Civic organizations previously had to explain the advantages of cooperating and working together; the case no longer needs to be made. The discussion now is how and to what extent to cooperate. Metropolis 2020 has been effective in bringing other civic groups engaged in similar policy issues together and eliciting business perspectives and expertise on the issues. It fulfills a coordinating function and adds a strong advocacy voice. It does not attempt to take over issues or ignore other groups involved in the same issues but instead seeks to work with them to maximize efforts.[24] Metropolis 2020 also facilitates organization or development of other civic agencies or coalitions. For example, it is making available office space and some administrative assistance to Business Leaders for Transportation, a joint venture of the MPC, the Chicagoan Chamber of Commerce, and Metropolis 2020.

Business and civic leadership in Chicago has been mobilized and energized by Metropolis 2020, but much of the suburban leadership is still skeptical and in open opposition to some of the goals of the organization.[25] Critics complain that Metropolis 2020 leaders do not understand how things work in the suburbs or understand the political implications involved in regional issues. It may also be that the suburbs are left out because they are not well organized and do not have a unified leadership that can speak for them in the same way that business and civic organizations can represent Chicago's interests. In any event, so far the problems addressed by Metropolis 2020 either have been largely Chicago problems or are championed by volunteer leaders more oriented to the city.

A recent goal-setting exercise is an example of the top-down, business-driven nature of the organization. The purpose of the exercise was to establish a set of ten goals and ways to measure progress toward them. The staff would then prepare a periodic report (on the order of a regional report card or regional indicators report) on progress toward achieving the ten goals. In preparation for the exercise, the staff distilled twenty-eight goals from the Chicago Metropolis 2020 report and held eight forums, four in the city and four in the suburbs. Each forum was cosponsored by an organization active in the particular geographical area. Attendance was by invitation only, with the majority of those invited from the lists of the cosponsoring organization. In addition to the more than five hundred people who attended the forums, more than fourteen hundred people were surveyed by mail. In each forum, participants reacted to the twenty-eight goals, refined them, and established their ten priorities.

After all the forums were completed, Metropolis 2020 staff, in conjunction with an advisory committee, combined similar goals and finalized the performance measures. In the process of combining similar goals and developing performance measures, the priority composite list developed through the forums was altered to reflect the agenda of Metropolis 2020. For example, early childhood education was nineteenth on the composite list but is prominently featured as one of the two goals under education to be measured in the regional indicators report. It also forms a major action item for Metropolis 2020 staff. The second highest priority from the forums was the need for sufficient fiscal capacity on the part of municipal governments to provide quality services. This was left off the goals to be measured by the regional report card.

The forums were obviously helpful in giving Metropolis 2020 visibility and having participants think about regional issues. However, if the objective was to reach out to the public and obtain meaningful input on goal development, the forums did not accomplish their purpose. They were one-shot efforts and did not create any lasting participant support. In fact, some participants felt that the forums were simply a mechanism for the organization to claim public support for its goals. In addition, the likelihood that the region could agree on ten priorities that would be acceptable for the entire area was probably never great to begin with. Moreover, because of substantial variation across the region, even the notion of a regional report card is problematic.

It would appear that the Chicago business community is using the successful Joint Venture: Silicon Valley as a model for Metropolis 2020. Joint Venture is a business-led organization involved in regional public policy issues. Both organizations have the support of top leadership of the area on their governing board, have a small staff, and work mainly through task forces. In addition, the executives of both organizations are well connected in the political and business establishments. However, there is a major difference between Metropolis 2020 and Joint Venture in the process and the extent of participation. Both produced a guiding report, but the Metropolis 2020 report was a product of the business community with little input from the community at large. Silicon Valley produced its guiding report through an extensive, participatory, interactive strategic planning process that involved more than one thousand people and took nine months to complete. Unlike the reaction to the Metropolis 2020 report, there was extensive commitment to the Joint Venture report and eagerness within the community to work on its implementation.[26] Moreover, the process in Silicon Valley continues to be much more participatory than it is in Chicago. The forums were the major effort at participation by Metropolis 2020. There is no evidence that the organization has a strategy or process to elicit further community participation.

Conclusion

The Chicago region possesses many of the criteria identified in this article that successful regional efforts exhibit. There is an active civic sector to promote networking and action on regional issues. The civic organization devoted to regional issues has the support and active involvement of leaders from businesses prominent in the Chicago region. There is a recently established regional mayor's organization, which indicates that the public leaders in the region recognize the need to cooperate and work together.

There are, however, a number of concerns. The active civic sector basically ends at Chicago city limits; the richness of the civic sector does not extend into the suburbs. The regional effort appears to be too narrowly focused on public policy issues that are of benefit to or a major concern for only certain areas of the region. There is concern that the civic organization is not addressing more important regional issues, those resulting from its own goal-setting process. The lack of broad participation in its decision-making process also raises the question as to its real intention. This is especially a concern on the part of suburban leaders, who see mainly a Chicago-focused agenda.

One element of successful effort in other metropolitan areas is the occurrence of a crisis or opportunity that helps drive change. So far, Metropolis 2020 has not made a convincing case that change is necessary, or even desirable. The organization has been successful in convincing the state government on some issues, but for its long-term viability it must educate the public and local political leaders about needs or opportunities that require regional solutions. Metropolis 2020 must also expand the involvement and participation of others in the community. It cannot be perceived to be business-dominated or central city–oriented. It should be viewed as a neutral, objective agency interested in bringing all stakeholders together to facilitate solutions to regional public policy problems. The process becomes extremely important in this context. Metropolis 2020 should focus on the process of involvement and develop and follow a strategic plan. Finally, there must be more collaboration with local political leaders from the region.

According to studies of regionalism, both the public and private sectors must work together for regional governance to be successful. The Metropolitan Mayors Caucus is a good parallel organization to Metropolis 2020. Each sector has made a commitment to regionalism by establishing a high-profile organization that brings its leaders together in regular meetings. Top business leaders are meeting and talking to one another about regional policy issues as they have not done in decades. The region's mayors are meeting regularly and talking and working together on regional issues as they have probably never done before. To the extent these two organizations can coalesce and talk and work together, real regional collaboration can occur. In fact, there is some movement in this direction. The caucus has started a dialogue with a civic organization on affordable housing issues; it has also appointed one of its members to an advisory committee of World Business Chicago, a civic organization that is charged with developing an international marketing strategy for the region. Furthermore, the caucus is partnering with a nonprofit group to seek a state grant to develop an economic development information system for the region.

Although the mayors caucus has made some effort to partner with the private sector, Metropolis 2020 has not been part of the initial collaboration effort. Metropolis 2020 needs to reach out to the public sector. If new regionalism is to be successful in the Chicago region, Metropolis 2020 has to take a leadership role. To do this, however, it must change how it does business. To the extent that it can retain the commitment and involvement of top business leadership; shed its business-driven, Chicago-oriented image; open up its processes; and become a broad-based, participant organization, it will be successful as a catalyst and leader in regional governance.

Appendix: List of Metropolitan Mayors Caucus Task Forces, Support Staff, Purposes, and Accomplishments

Commonwealth Edison Task Force. Membership: mayors, managers, Chicago Department of Environment

Purpose: to maintain an ongoing dialogue on electrical issues with Commonwealth Edison

Work product to date:

- Advocacy on electrical deregulation legislation
- Open line of communication with Interstate Commerce Commission
- Impact on reliability rules interpretation
- Developed strategic communication and capital development plan for suburban communities

Clean Air Task Force. Membership: mayors, managers, Department of Environment staff

Purpose: to develop a regional strategy for clean air

Work product to date:

- Secured funding to establish a regional alternative fueling station network
- With assistance of the International City/County Management Association, prepared a resource book identifying strategies and practices to promote clean air
- Established regional dialogue to include business, civic, and environmental groups in the process
- Formulating a regional clean air credit trading bank

Economic Development Task Force. Membership: mayors, economic development specialist, Chicago's Department of Planning staff

Purpose: to formulate a regional economic development agenda that affects development of the statewide economic development plan
Work product to date:

- Secured $100,000 in grant funds to hire an economic development expert to guide the process
- Identifying commonly shared economic development needs among the more than two hundred mayors of the Metropolitan Mayors Caucus
- Reviewing and inventorying the existing and pending activities of economic development–oriented organizations throughout Metro Chicago
- Identifying U.S. best practices in regional economic development and in local and state cooperation and coordination (potential models for Metro Chicago)
- Articulating a progressive economic development agenda on behalf of mayors throughout Metro Chicago
- Enabled the Metropolitan Mayors Caucus to speak as one voice for the region to influence the state's strategic planning efforts for economic development

Legislative Chairs Task Force. Membership: chairpersons of the legislative committees of the participating conferences, and staff from the City of Chicago's Department of Intergovernmental Affairs
Purpose: to determine joint legislative positions and strategies
Work product to date:

- Passed legislation requiring Commonwealth Edison to submit emergency plans for municipal approval
- Instrumental in passage of Illinois First
- Promoted gun legislation and continued strategy

Smart Growth Task Force. Membership: mayors, managers, City of Chicago's chief of policy
Purpose: to develop a consensus position on smart-growth issues, initiatives
Work product to date:

- Development of regional vision statement
- Development of smart-growth municipal principles

Y2K Task Force. Membership: MIS directors, municipal staff
Purpose: to ensure regional review and coordination of Y2K issues
Work product to date:

- Exchange of individual municipal response plans
- Preparation for regional Y2K White House conversation

Notes

1. Wallis, A. D. "The Third Wave: Current Trends in Regional Governance." *National Civic Review,* 1994, *83* (3), 289–305.

2. Interviews were conducted for this article with sixteen people involved with Metropolis, the mayors caucus, and other regional organizations. All were guaranteed anonymity. The interviews were conducted during the months of October and November 2000.

3. Committee for Economic Development. *Modernizing Local Government.* New York: Committee for Economic Development, 1966.

4. Putnam, R. D. *Making Democracy Work: Civic Traditions in Modern Italy.* Princeton, N.J.: Princeton University Press, 1993.

5. Henton, D., Melville, J., and Walesh, K. *Grassroots Leaders for a New Economy: How Civic Entrepreneurs Are Building Prosperous Communities.* San Francisco: Jossey-Bass, 1997.

6. Lyall, K. "A Bicycle Built for Two: Public-Private Partnership in Baltimore." In R. S. Fosler and R. A. Berger (eds.), *Public-Private Partnership in American Cities: Seven Case Studies.* Lexington, Mass.: Heath, 1982.

7. Foster, K. A. "The Privatization of Regionalism." Paper presented at the annual meeting of the Urban Affairs Association, New York, Mar. 1996.

8. Henton, Melville, and Walesh (1997); Henton, D., Melville, J., and Walesh, K. "The New Economic Geography of America's Regions: How the New Economy Makes Place Important Today." *Regionalist,* 1997, 2 (4), 21–25.

9. Sjoquist, D. L. "The Legacy of the 1996 Olympics." *Regionalist,* 1997, 2 (1), 12–17.

10. Owen, C. J., and Willbern, Y. *Governing Metropolitan Indianapolis: The Politics of Unigov.* Berkeley and Los Angeles: University of California Press, 1985.

11. Brandl, J., and Brooks, R. "Public-Private Cooperation for Urban Revitalization: The Minneapolis and Saint Paul Experience." In R. S. Fosler and R. A. Berger (eds.), *Public-Private Partnership in American Cities: Seven Case Studies.* Lexington, Mass.: Heath, 1982.

12. Peirce, N. "Citizen Groups on Vanguard of Civic Renewal." *Arlington Heights* [Ill.] *Daily Herald,* Dec. 30, 1996, sect. 1, p. 12.

13. Hershberg, T., Magidson, P., and Wernecke, M. L. "Promoting Regional Cooperation in Southeastern Pennsylvania." *National Civic Review,* 1992, 81 (4), 418–434.

14. Chrislip, D. D., and Larson, C. E. *Collaborative Leadership: How Citizens and Civic Leaders Can Make a Difference.* San Francisco: Jossey-Bass, 1994.

15. Mazmanian, D., and Stanley-Jones, M. "Strategies II: Reconceiving LULUs: Changing the Nature and Scope of Locally Unwanted Land Uses." In J. F. DiMento and L. Graymer (eds.), *Confronting Regional Challenges: Approaches to LULUs, Growth, and Other Vexing Governance Problems.* Cambridge, Mass.: Lincoln Institute of Land Policy, 1991.

16. Weir, M. "Central Cities' Loss of Power in State Politics." *Cityscape: A Journal of Policy Development and Research,* 1996, 2 (2), 23–32.

17. Mahtesian, C. "Semi-Vendetta: Cities and the New Republican Order." *Governing,* 1996, 9 (6), 28–30.

18. Mahtesian (1996).

19. Weir, M. "Coalition Building for Regionalism." In B. Katz (ed.), *Reflections on Regionalism.* Washington, D.C.: Brookings Institution Press, 2000.

20. Pearson, R. "Chicago Now Second City to Its Suburbs." In "Chicago: A Work in Progress," *Chicago Tribune* Special Reprint, published originally Feb. 7–14, 1999.

21. Johnson, E. W. *Chicago Metropolis 2020.* Chicago: Commercial Club of Chicago, 1999. The Commercial Club is the most prestigious civic organization in Chicago. It is composed of top-echelon business leaders from the major business firms in the Chicago region. Its membership is by invitation only.

22. In addition to Ranney and his considerable influence with state and Chicago political leaders, other notable executive volunteers are Paula Wolfe, retired president of Governors

State University; Adele Simmons, retired president of the MacArthur Foundation; Whitney Addington, former chief of medicine at Rush-Presbyterian Hospital; and King Harris, president and chief executive officer of Pittway Corporation.

23. Even a token member can be valuable to the purposes of the organization if he or she chooses to become involved. For example, the union member mobilized his constituency to assist in passage of Illinois First legislation.

24. An example of Metropolis's role in working with other agencies is an early childhood education effort. Metropolis leaders met with early childhood groups to determine how they could help. The groups indicated they needed state legislation that would provide additional resources. Metropolis required the groups to justify their numbers and show the likely impact of the additional resources. The advocacy groups worked together in developing a united proposal; Metropolis then coordinated an advocacy and education campaign with the state legislature to obtain passage of the legislation.

25. An overarching metropolitan council the likes of the Twin Cities Metropolitan Council and tax revenue sharing, to name two goals encountering considerable opposition.

26. Henton, Melville, and Walesh (1997).

David K. Hamilton is professor of public administration at Roosevelt University in Chicago.

The National Civic Congress: A Proposal for Movement Building

Carmen Sirianni, Lewis A. Friedland

In 1992, John Gardner spent much of the year looking at community build-ing efforts around the country and found himself astonished at the amount of good work going on. In the decade since, it has now become clear that Gardner was on to something very important. Not only has there been a sig-nificant amount of civic innovation occurring in various arenas, but a civic renewal movement has emerged that seeks to link them and revitalize American democracy for the twenty-first century. Gardner and his colleagues at the National Civic League, along with other organizational partners, have been among those with the vision to build this movement.

The civic renewal movement inherits some of the energy of past move-ments for participatory democracy and civic inclusion, such as the civil rights and women's movements, but it is also different in important respects. Draw-ing from new sources of energy and inspiration, the civic renewal movement has produced innovative forms of civic practice for dealing with complex pub-lic problems and collaboration among diverse social actors. But the distinc-tiveness of this movement means that its development is likely to differ from many of the movements for rights and social justice of recent decades. It is cer-tainly possible that the civic renewal movement will stall before gaining the kind of visibility and power that make a real difference in American civic, polit-ical, and institutional life.

In this article, we outline a proposal for building a civic renewal move-ment that can draw upon the strengths of its distinctive repertoires while over-coming some of the inherent obstacles such a movement faces. At the core of our proposal is a National Civic Congress, which would convene annually or biennially around the Fourth of July. It would assemble hundreds, even thou-sands, of teams of citizens whose collaborative public work and community problem solving might be used to instruct the broader public and our politi-cal and institutional leaders in the diverse yet practical methods of civic democracy available for renewing the foundations of self-government. It would bring together in a common project many of the organizations working in disparate arenas to develop innovative models. But before elaborating on this, let us first sketch the outlines of the emerging movement and some of the obstacles confronting it.

The Civic Renewal Movement

Movements almost never begin with a well-defined identity or widely accepted label. Rather, they emerge over years, even decades, from many forms of local action that only gradually—and often begrudgingly—begin to use a common language, form cross-cutting networks, and identify as a movement having widely recognized goals for political or social transformation.

The civic renewal movement is no different. Its roots can be found in such organizations as Save the Bay in Rhode Island, which transformed itself from an advocacy organization in the 1970s to one that combined advocacy and policy development with broad civic education and hands-on restoration of a large watershed by its many stakeholders. The movement draws inspiration from the methods developed by Communities Organized for Public Service and Metro Alliance in San Antonio, as these groups learned how to leverage their protest capacity into long-term civic partnership among congregations, schools, banks, employers, and public officials to support community development, school reform, and job training for poor and working class Mexican American and African American communities.

The civic renewal movement springs up on college campuses, such as the University of Pennsylvania, when professors gain the support of the university president to forge lasting partnerships with community groups, congregations, unions, and businesses to improve neighborhoods and schools and to engage university students in the work of revitalization through some eighty service learning courses. The movement finds resonance in the newsroom of the *Charlotte Observer*, for instance, when editors and reporters decide to cover crime in a way that engages communities—black and white, middle-class and poor—in deliberating about underlying causes and mapping out collaborative solutions. The movement manifests itself when youth agencies such as ROCA (Reaching Out to Chelsea Adolescents) in Massachusetts develop "peacemaking circles" to engage youths in violence reduction and health promotion, and it builds partnerships with city and state agencies, whose staff also participate in the circles.

Cities such as Portland, Oregon, are fertile ground for the civic renewal movement, as the Office of Neighborhood Involvement there facilitates the work of neighborhood associations and other civic groups in community problem solving, the planning office engages citizens in land-use planning, the Bureau of Environmental Services works with watershed and neighborhood associations and schools in ecosystem restoration, the police department develops extensive community policing, the district attorney's office employs "neighborhood DAs" to assist citizens in crime prevention, the Multnomah County Youth Advisory Board facilitates youth engagement, and Portland State University and Portland Community College rethink their mission and embrace the goal of developing engaged citizens to further build the civic capacities of these and many other kinds of institution.

In each arena, as our recently published *Civic Innovation in America* and our forthcoming *The Youth of Our Democracy* show,[1] there is not only local innovation but also formation or transformation of local, state, and national networks. These networks have increasingly come to speak a common language of "community building," "collaborative problem solving," "public work," "democratic deliberation," "relationship building," and "consensus seeking." Many borrow methods and tools from one another, such as community visioning, study circles, one-on-ones, asset mapping, and the *Civic Index* (a tool developed by the National Civic League). There has been considerable proliferation of toolkits and best-practice manuals in recent years to help guide civic action. In various arenas, local innovators and national networks—many of whom have hundreds and in some cases even several thousand organizational members or affiliates—have come to define their own movements with distinctive civic "frames," as social movement theorists call them. A brief and incomplete sketch of the movements and networks that have developed substantial or partial civic frames and strategies looks something like this; keep in mind there are different emphases and even competing models within each.

Watershed Movement. *Frame.* Although regulation is important, command-and-control regulation is not enough to protect and restore watersheds and ecosystems. Civic associations (watershed associations, councils, alliances, and "friends of the stream" groups, along with neighborhood associations, land trusts, schools, and fishing and boating clubs) need to engage directly in monitoring and restoration; forge consensus with farmers, ranchers, and other business stakeholders; and work collaboratively with agencies that help build civic capacity. "Watershed democracy" helps reconceptualize the locus and means of democratic action.

Networks. River Network, Global Rivers Environmental Education Network, Izaak Walton League, Restore America's Estuaries, River Watch Network, National Audubon Society, and Nature Conservancy, along with regional and state groups such as Chesapeake Bay Alliance, Massachusetts Watershed Coalition, and Rivers Council of Washington. The ecosystem restoration movement and sustainable communities movement share similar perspectives and include still other organizational networks; the environmental justice movement now includes many civic partnership models.[2]

Community Development, Congregation-Based Organizing, and Community Building Movements. *Frame.* Though there are many federal and state programs and social service agencies that can help reduce poverty and promote urban development, sustainable strategies require much greater emphasis on engaging local residents, congregations, and civic organizations in building new sources of power, mobilizing community assets, forging sustainable partnerships, and developing common vision. Bricks-and-mortar in community development must be combined with social capital, community building, and civic engagement.

Networks. Industrial Areas Foundation (IAF); National Community Building Network; Assets-Based Community Development Institute; Neighborhoods USA; Center for Community Change; Study Circles Resource Center; Pew Partnership for Civic Change; National Civic League; and National League of Cities.[3]

Civic Engagement Movement in Higher Education. *Frame.* Colleges and universities contribute to democracy in many important ways, but narrowly specialized professional and disciplinary cultures must be reexamined in light of how institutions of higher learning do and do not nurture the skills and commitments of active citizenship among students, faculty, administrators, staff, and surrounding communities. Service learning, participatory action research, university-community partnership, and sustainable campus projects are among the various forms for engaging campus and community stakeholders in renewing the civic mission of higher education.

Networks. Campus Compact, along with its affiliated state compacts and its National Center for Community Colleges; American Association for Higher Education; American Association of Community Colleges; Center for Democracy and Citizenship; National Society for Experiential Education; Council of Independent Colleges; New England Resource Center for Higher Education; Campus Ecology Program of the National Wildlife Federation; and the newly formed Association for Community and Higher Education Partnerships.[4]

Healthy Communities Movement. *Frame.* Medical care is just one of the many formal and informal community resources that contribute to building a healthy community. Others are cultural norms that support healthy behaviors; public safety, adequate housing, and recreation; family supports, social capital, and faith communities; and education and living-wage jobs. Strategies for improving long-term health in the broadest sense, especially of disadvantaged communities, must empower people as civic actors and nurture partnership among civic associations, congregations, medical institutions, public health agencies, universities, and other institutions charged with broad community development.

Networks. Coalition for Healthier Cities and Communities; state- and citywide healthy communities coalitions; National Civic League; Hospital Research Education Trust; Carter Center/Emory University Interfaith Health Program and its Health and Faith Consortia in five cities; Health Ministries Association; and parish nursing associations.[5]

Civic Journalism and Public Journalism Movement. *Frame.* Journalists cannot remain content with the usual routines of horse race coverage of elections, polarized framing of issues, or disinterested objectivity. Professional norms of objectivity can be combined with new (and old) reporting practices that help constitute vital publics with the usable knowledge that enables them to deliberate about complex issues, map their community's own assets, understand successful strategies in other communities, and engage in common problem solving. Journalists can facilitate democracy in the way they help constitute the public sphere and hold all institutional actors, including citizens themselves, accountable.

Networks. Pew Center for Civic Journalism; Kettering Foundation; Public Broadcasting System's Democracy Project and National Center for Outreach; Association of Educators in Journalism and Mass Communication; and Harwood Group.[6]

Community Youth Development Movement. *Frame.* Young people are not primarily problems to be fixed or clients to be served but instead have developmental assets and civic skills that can be nurtured so as to enable them to make a real contribution to the community and institutions today, not just when they become adults. They can contribute through service in school and community—in environmental restoration, crime prevention, public health campaigns, youth-run teen courts, antiracism and sexual discrimination work, and young women's empowerment projects. They can help set the agenda on city youth commissions, such as those in San Francisco and Hampton, Virginia, and on the board of agencies and nonprofits. Young people are capable of sustained public work in partnership with adults and institutions, not just through intermittent or individual volunteerism.

Networks. National Network for Youth, Innovation Center for Community and Youth Development, Forum for Youth Investment, YouthBuild USA, National 4-H Council, YMCA, Center for Democracy and Citizenship, Do Something, National Youth Advocacy Coalition, and Center for Youth and Communities and its *CYD Journal.*[7]

Service Learning Movement in K–12 Schools. *Frame.* Too many schools are failing to nurture the skills and values of active citizenship either by neglecting civic education completely or by offering it in a stale pedagogical format. This poses a threat to the long-term vitality of democracy. Students should be offered courses that engage them in active service and problem solving in the community and simultaneously enable them to reflect systematically on community issues and democratic skills as a core part of academic learning.

Networks. Learning in Deed, National Alliance for Civic Education, North American Association for Environmental Education, Education Commission of the States, Center for Civic Education, Constitutional Rights Foundation, and Center for Information and Research on Civic Learning and Engagement (CIRCLE).[8]

Community Justice Movement. *Frame.* The detached professional model and rapid-response practices of policing are not especially effective at reducing crime. Greater emphasis must be placed on decentralized communication with the community, broadly focused problem solving, citizen definition of conditions that breed fear and foster crime, and "coproduction of safety" by citizens and their local associations. Methods include beat meetings, neighborhood watches, community and teen courts, family violence courts, and neighborhood DAs.

Networks. Community Policing Consortium (International Association of Chiefs of Police, National Organization of Black Law Enforcement Executives, National Sheriff's Association, Police Executive Research Forum, Police Foundation), Youth Crime Watch of America, and National Youth Court Center.[9]

Forging Links Among the Frames

In some arenas, these frames have been partially incorporated into policy design and agency practice, as with the Environmental Protection Agency's support for community-based environmental protection, Department of Justice programs for community policing and teen courts, Housing and Urban Development's office for university-community partnerships, the Corporation for National Service support for service learning and AmeriCorps, state adoption of watershed strategies, and city designs for Beacon Schools and youth commissions.

The work that the civic renewal movement has set for itself is to forge stronger links among these various networks and organizations and to develop what social movement theorists call an "elaborated master frame"[10] that can build upon, enrich, and encompass the civic frames that are being generated in each arena so that their work can be leveraged to a new level and inspire broad democratic revitalization.

Thus we see the Alliance for National Renewal fashion a set of general principles and build a network of several hundred organizations. We see the Center for Democracy and Citizenship convene civic and government leaders around the Reinventing Citizenship Project and fashion a *Civic Declaration* that has been distributed widely, and the National Commission on Civic Renewal develop general themes for a civic renewal movement. We see the Kettering Foundation foster an array of initiatives and research spanning various institutional spheres, and the civic and academic leaders who came together in the Saguaro Seminar at Harvard University develop a set of proposals for regenerating social capital in diverse settings.

Our own Youth Civic Engagement Project has been convening innovative practitioners and youth leaders from different arenas to explore strategies for building a broad and highly visible youth civic engagement movement, which is part of a larger set of projects supported by the Pew Charitable Trusts. Crosscutting leadership networks run through all of these national efforts.[11]

Barriers to Building a Movement

Needless to say, there are many barriers to civic practice and policy design taking deeper root in each of these arenas,[12] and formidable obstacles to building a broad movement that weaves them together fruitfully and sustainably. Here we wish to focus briefly on some of the latter obstacles, in the interest of developing a proposal for movement building that can address them effectively.

First, it is essential to emphasize that, although important leaders in each of the arenas we have mentioned recognize the need for broader civic revitalization and identify with the emerging civic renewal movement, many others do not yet see the connections, have never even heard of a civic renewal movement, or do not generally come into contact with civic innovators from other arenas. In the six hundred interviews we have conducted with practitioners over the past eight years, however, we found a great deal of enthusiasm for the idea of being part of a larger movement and sharing perspectives with those in other areas of work, since this yields hope that their own work might be more broadly recognized and gain the support that it needs—and since the idea of a broader movement is consistent with their own underlying democratic vision and values. There is, consequently, much potential, but much that still needs to be done in nurturing the connections.

Second, leaders in each arena are rightly focused on the work in their specific institution, community, and intermediary organization; they have limited time and resources to devote to building a broader movement. Some may support the latter in principle, but this does not mean that they are willing to go to still more meetings or devote scarce organizational resources to activities peripheral to their core mission—whether it be restoring a watershed, revitalizing an inner-city community, rethinking the civic mission of a university, or doing the training and policy work that can support these activities. Movement-building activities must therefore have modest costs and clear benefits if we are to attract an array of organizations.

Third, although the civic renewal movement builds upon many of the democratic achievements of recent movements for civil rights and social justice, it is not a rights or justice movement per se. Because it seeks to foster new forms of civic collaboration and public work among groups that may differ on important issues, it cannot use the repertoire of many recent movements. It cannot inspire action on the basis of unconditional claims to rights or a righteous struggle against a clearly defined oppressor. It cannot invoke a metaphor of unambiguous good and evil or moral resistance in the face of power. It cannot capture and focus public attention through mass protest, marches on Washington, boycotts, strikes, freedom rides, and sit-ins, nor can it count on repression by authorities to galvanize widespread support. It cannot expect dramatic court decisions to energize activists or secure significant new levers of power and representation. It lacks a constitutional amendment—such as what the Equal Rights Amendment accomplished for the women's movement—around which to organize to guarantee the power and responsibility of citizens to practice effective self-government. Legislation can certainly enact policy designs that help build civic capacity in specific arenas; but as we have indicated, a broadly based civic renewal movement cutting across many institutional sectors cannot hope to build its networks through advocacy coalition and lobbying for specific laws.[13]

National Civic Congress: Reclaiming the
Fourth of July for Self–Government

To help build the civic renewal movement in light of these constraints, we offer a proposal for a National Civic Congress. This event would convene hundreds, and eventually thousands, of teams of citizens whose collaborative work has made a significant contribution to public life and whose methods of community problem solving are especially instructive and inspiring to the nation. The congress would convene annually or biennially in Washington, D.C., and eventually in state capitals and other cities and towns as well, on or around the weekend of the Fourth of July in a festive celebration of self-governance that claims cultural authority for the civic models in our political culture and challenges political and institutional leaders to lend their support to building civic capacity further. This July congress would bring heightened visibility and nurture common identity among those organizations and civic movements operating in diverse arenas; they would serve as the key partners in selecting the delegate teams.

Our proposal is admittedly ambitious, though not, we trust, inappropriately so in view of the great challenge of democratic renewal. Clearly, it is neither politically nor organizationally utopian, even if it does call for the broad circle of movement leaders to take a bold step forward together. Indeed, many of the networks we have mentioned already do some version of this at their conferences, but they rarely do it with other networks outside their own arena or with broad movement building goals or high visibility. Let us elaborate on some of the possible components.

Civic Action Teams Tell Stories of Renewal. The core component of the July congress would be teams of civic activists telling stories of renewal that are ongoing in communities, workplaces, and institutions across the country. Storytelling, part of the venerable social movement repertoire of bearing witness, can take many forms, but it should establish the dignity and satisfaction of public work, the diversity and availability of practical models, and the commitment to continue the difficult task of learning in the messy world of collaboration and democracy.

Through the civic congress, teams of citizen delegates who have worked in innovative partnerships—which includes everyone from ordinary neighborhood activists, students, union stewards, and congregation members to professionals, civil servants, business managers, and elected office holders—assume the responsibility for educating the nation in the arts of civic democracy. They bear witness to working through conflict to reach enough common ground to enable them to produce things of genuine public value. They testify to building relationships of trust to serve them in their future work. They claim the cultural authority and civic responsibility to meet the challenge that Thomas Jefferson laid down in the early days of the republic, which is no less relevant today and will be no less critical as far as the democratic eye can see into the future: "I know of no safe repository of the ultimate powers of the society but the people themselves; and if we think them not enlightened enough to exercise control with a wholesome discretion, the remedy is not to take it from them, but to inform their discretion by education." Democracy is an art that must be learned and relearned, especially in an increasingly complex world. Through its July gathering, the movement thus assumes a singularly visible role as a congress of civic educators in the unfinished and imperfect, yet no less noble, work of democracy.

Teams of delegates might be chosen in various ways. We place special emphasis on national, state, and local intermediaries nominating those teams that they consider to be doing exemplary and especially instructive work. Some already give awards that could help selection, such as the National Civic League's All America City awards; Neighborhoods USA's Neighborhood of the Year awards; Chesapeake Bay Partner Communities awards; Pew Center for Civic Journalism's Batten awards; Campus Compact's Ehrlich awards; and many similar awards in community planning, youth leadership, and program innovation. Scholars, agency professionals, and funders have still other compendia of best cases from which selection can be made. As the venue of the July congress expands from Washington to communities around the country, the process of selection can be opened up much further.

Practitioners and Scholars Explore Policy Designs That Build Civic Capacity. If practical stories of renewal are recounted by teams of citizen delegates in a way that makes them accessible and inspiring to a broad public, the July congress can also include in-depth critical exchange on key models and policy designs, as well as scholarly analysis of general trends and benchmarks of civic health. Policy design is absolutely essential to renewal—if not in every area of civic life, then certainly in those where citizens engage with complex institutional systems and produce complex public goods such as sustainable ecosystems, community health, or safe communities. Democracy in contemporary America cannot be revitalized unless policy making itself aims to nurture the virtues of democratic citizenship and the capacities of civic problem solving. A diverse and nonpartisan movement that does not have available a lobbying and advocacy coalition strategy ought nonetheless to help focus public attention and debate on policy designs that tend to foster democracy, in contrast to those that do not.

The July congress can draw upon the familiar repertoire of academic and policy conferences, but it can also bring practitioners and lawmakers into the discussion to build networks oriented toward mutual education and ongoing action. Thus, for example, a general session on civic environmentalism might include the National Academy of Public Administration, which has produced important reports to Congress; it might invite key congressional committee and staff members, EPA officials, policy intellectuals, and a range of innovators from watershed councils, state government, sustainable city projects, environmental groups, business, and civic associations. To foster incisive critical reflection, identify key obstacles and limits, and develop relationships that might prove essential to later work, the session could also include skeptics and opponents of collaborative approaches.

Even though consensus on a policy agenda would not be the purpose of this particular session or of the July congress as a whole, participants could explore a range of options for effective advocacy through other channels. A similar format could be followed for specific environmental policy design sessions on watersheds, forests, toxics, and sustainable cities, and for other broad policy arenas, such as community development, health, family, aging, education, and work.

Practitioner Groups Display Their Wares and Market Their Services. If an essential part of civic renewal is enabling an organization to access useful models and best practices that have been tried elsewhere, the July congress can help give definition and publicity to the marketplace of tools and services that various intermediaries can offer. This can be done through display booths and workshops that have the flavor of a grand civic fair—one need only attend an All America City Awards meeting to get a sense of the incredible spirit that can be generated at such an event.

It can also be done through a coordinated marketing strategy among the gathering's partners and sponsors, including comprehensive print, CD-ROM, and Web-based guides to publications and videos; training services; organizational affiliation; funding sources; degree programs; career opportunities; and agency programs that support civic skill building and public work. This would be particularly useful to younger people looking to identify pathways for sustained engagement beyond their initial experiences and to groups on the periphery of major networks. Indeed, one of the key rationales for organizing a National Civic Congress would be to regularly map the civic marketplace through collaboration of a range of groups. The stories, case studies, and other presentations by the delegate teams and guests could serve to develop further video, CD-ROM, and other learning resources for the civic marketplace.[14]

Citizens Challenge Elected Officials to Provide Real Support for Civic Problem-Solving Models. Since the July congress is designed as a claim to cultural authority for democratic public work and collaborative problem solving within American politics, it would be important to invite elected officials to attend the sessions, recount to the delegates and broader public what they may have learned, and express their own commitment to similar modes of civic action and government support. The July congress would aim to establish and publicize as a basic norm of politics that government officials have no more important task than to facilitate the democratic work of citizens themselves. Current and former public officials from both parties who have a proven record of working with innovative civic partnerships—and there are many of them all across the country who would be honored to attend—would lend added legitimacy to the efforts of the July congress to establish this norm.

But the circle needs to be broadened and the challenge made more poignant. Thus, the July congress might use a variant of the Industrial Areas Foundation's accountability nights by inviting the president and the leader of the opposition party in Congress—or, during an election year, the presumed nominees or leading candidates for president—to tell how their own policies and governing philosophies will enable the work of citizens to flourish. They would be welcomed to share in the symbolic value of the July congress and its celebration of self-government, but only to the extent that they engage its themes and the work of its delegates with a seriousness that goes beyond the usual platitudes of a Fourth of July speech.

Conclusion

A National Civic Congress would offer an opportunity for raising the visibility and establishing the cultural authority of public work and collaborative problem solving in American political culture. Stories of renewal that are part of a major political holiday celebrating self-governance could attract mainstream press coverage, cable news outlets, and C-Span. They could create an opportunity for public broadcasting partnership, as in *Citizens' State of the Union* in 1997, when some ten stations collaborating with local newspapers and radio stations under the leadership of Wisconsin Public Television aired national programs on major holidays, such as the Fourth of July, that were built around citizen frames. Stories of renewal can also be part of a coordinated media strategy by civic organizations and Websites themselves, and live Webcasts could cover the sessions.

Stories of renewal at the July congress would offer a powerful and inspiring image of teams of citizens from all walks of life and every corner of the country working collaboratively to solve the difficult problems that beset us amid all the messiness, conflict, uncertainty, and failure that a free people acting in an imperfect world invariably face. This is an image that has deep resonance among an overwhelmingly nonideological and pragmatic public; the response to the events of September 11 has further heightened the appeal of citizens collaborating for large public purpose.

The National Civic Congress would celebrate the work of citizens in building the commonwealth and thus lay claim to the symbolism of our nation's most important political holiday in order to renew self-government. As many other major movements throughout history have marked significant events by ritual practice and gathering, the July congress would reclaim a major national ritual for the civic renewal movement. For those so inclined, an ecumenical service would anchor the commitment to revitalize the civic foundations of the republic in the deepest and broadest traditions of those faith communities already hard at work.

A July congress can shape and firmly establish the identity of the civic renewal movement in the eyes of civic activists themselves, for whom the affinity of diverse civic models and movements could become much more evident. The key incentives that the July congress can offer to those inevitably concerned about how movement building contributes to their own specific work and justify a commitment of scarce time and resources are heightened visibility, increased legitimacy, and useful networks beyond those already available. As the legitimacy of civic approaches is enhanced, so would July congress participants likely receive further support in their particular arena. The barrier to entry for groups already engaged in civic work is relatively low, since participation in the July congress does not require agreement on a substantive programmatic agenda. Nor does participation require deployment of substantial new resources in a common project.

The disincentives to participate on the part of groups concerned with sharing the spotlight with too many other parallel projects or competing models would be effectively held in check by the desire not to be left out, especially once the July congress achieved a certain critical mass of participating groups and public recognition. In fact, in our discussion with leading practitioners on several occasions over the past months, there has been considerable enthusiasm for the idea of a civic congress; even those skeptical of the proposal said they would not refuse to bring a team if they were invited. The time commitment is modest—a few days of preparation and travel—and funding could help defray the costs. Funding for such efforts now has several precedents: the National Commission on Civic Renewal, Alliance for National Renewal, *Citizens State of the Union,* National Issues Convention, and Presidents' Summit for America's Future. Resources can also be contributed by local projects and intermediaries themselves, or by those who fund specific projects, as is typically the case with such a gathering. Perhaps an endowment could be raised to make the July congress a permanent feature of our political culture and ceremony.[15]

The July congress offers the opportunity to build a movement in a way that signals large purpose while setting modest and achievable goals. It offers the rationale for identifying leaders in a progressively broader array of institutional arenas year in and year out, and for mapping an ever-richer assortment of innovative approaches. If the civic renewal movement cannot achieve identity and recognition by mass protests, freedom rides, and marches on Washington, the National Civic Congress can perhaps offer a functional equivalent to a march on Washington that can inspire and energize local action in the everyday public work and collaboration of a vital civic democracy.[16]

Notes

1. See Sirianni, C., and Friedland, L. *Civic Innovation in America: Community Empowerment, Public Policy, and the Movement for Civic Renewal.* Berkeley: University of California Press, 2001; and *The Youth of Our Democracy: Young Americans and the Democratic Work of the Republic* (forthcoming). Robert Putnam's analysis of the decline in aggregate measures of social capital, though largely correct in our opinion, generally misses evidence of civic innovation at the grass

roots and through various networks. See Putnam, R. *Bowling Alone: The Collapse and Revival of American Community.* New York: Simon and Schuster, 2000.

2. Shutkin, W. *The Land That Could Be: Environmentalism and Democracy in the Twenty-First Century.* Cambridge, Mass.: MIT Press, 2000; Landy, M. K., Susman, M. M., and Knopman, D. S. *Civic Environmentalism in Action: A Field Guide to Regional and Local Initiatives.* Washington, D.C.: Progressive Policy Institute, Jan. 1999; and Sirianni and Friedland (2001), chapter three.

3. Shirley, D. *Community Organizing for Urban School Reform.* Austin: University of Texas Press, 1997; Warren, M. R. *Dry Bones Rattling: Community Building to Revitalize American Democracy.* Princeton: Princeton University Press, 2001; Berry, J., Portney, K., and Thomson, K. *The Rebirth of Urban Democracy.* Washington, D.C.: Brookings, 1993; Kingsley, G. T., McNeely, J., and Gibson, J. *Community Building: Coming of Age.* Baltimore: Development Training Institute and Urban Institute, 1997; and Sirianni and Friedland (2001), chapter two.

4. Ehrlich, T. (ed.). *Civic Responsibility and Higher Education.* Phoenix: Oryx Press, 2000; Bringle, R., Games, R., and Malloy, E. A. (eds.). *Colleges and Universities as Citizens.* Needham Heights, Mass.: Allyn and Bacon, 1999; Maurasse, D. J. *Beyond the Campus: How Colleges and Universities Form Partnerships with Their Communities.* New York: Routledge, 2001.

5. Duhl, L., and Lee, P. (eds.). "Focus on Healthy Communities." (Special double issue.) *Public Health Reports,* Mar.–Apr. and May–June 2000, *115,* 2–3; Johnson, K., Grossman, W., and Cassidy, A. (eds.). *Collaborating to Improve Community Health: Workbook and Guide to Best Practices in Creating Healthier Communities and Populations.* San Francisco: Jossey-Bass, 1996; Bogue, R., and Hall, C., Jr. (eds.). *Health Network Innovations: How 20 Communities Are Improving Their Systems Through Collaboration.* Chicago: American Hospital Publishing, 1997; and Sirianni and Friedland (2001), chapter four.

6 . Rosen, J. *What Are Journalists for?* New Haven: Yale University Press, 1999; Merritt, D. *Public Journalism and Public Life: Why Telling the News Is Not Enough.* Hillsdale, N.J.: Erlbaum, 1995; Glasser, T. (ed.). *The Idea of Public Journalism.* New York: Guilford, 1999; and Sirianni and Friedland (2001), chapter five.

7. Pittman, K., Ferber, T., and Irby, M. *Youth as Effective Citizens.* Takoma Park, Md.: International Youth Foundation–U.S., 2000; Zeldin, S., McDaniel, A. K., Topitzes, D., and Calvert, M. *Youth in Decision Making: A Study on the Impacts of Youth on Adults and Organizations.* Chevy Chase, Md.: National 4-H Council/Innovation Center for Community and Youth Development, 2000; and Sirianni, C., and others. "Community Youth Development and Civic Engagement Networks: Preliminary Mapping." Waltham, Mass.: Center for Youth and Communities, Brandeis University, Sept. 2001.

8. Stanton, T. K., Giles, D. E., and Cruz, N. I. *Service Learning: A Movement's Pioneers Reflect on Its Origins, Practice, and Future.* San Francisco: Jossey-Bass, 1999; Billig, S. H. "Research on K–12 School-Based Service Learning." *Phi Delta Kappan,* May 2000, pp. 658–664; Skinner, R., and Chapman, C. *Service Learning and Community Service in K–12 Public Schools.* Washington, D.C.: National Center for Educational Statistics, U.S. Department of Education, Sept. 1999.

9. Skogan, W., and Hartnett, S. *Community Policing, Chicago Style.* New York: Oxford University Press, 1997; Carp, D. R. *Community Justice: An Emerging Field.* Lanham, Md.: Rowman and Littlefield, 1998; Miller, S. L. *Gender and Community Policing: Walking the Talk.* Boston: Northeastern University Press, 1999.

10. See Snow, D., and Benford, R. "Master Frames and Cycles of Protest." In A. Morris and C. M. Mueller (eds.), *Frontiers in Social Movement Theory.* New Haven: Yale University Press, 1992; Snow, D., Rocheford, E. B., Jr., Worden, S., and Benford, R. "Frame Alignment Processes, Micromobilization, and Movement Participation." *American Sociological Review,* 1986, *51* (4), 464–481.

11. See the Final Report of the National Commission on Civic Renewal. *A Nation of Spectators: How Civic Disengagement Weakens America and What We Can Do About It.* College Park, Md.: National Commission on Civic Renewal, June 1998; Boyte, H., Barber, B., Marshall, W., and Sirianni, C. *Civic Declaration: A Call for a New Citizenship.* Dayton: Kettering Foundation, Dec. 1994; Gardner, J. *National Renewal.* Washington, D.C., and Denver: Independent Sector and

National Civic League, Sept. 1995; Alliance for National Renewal. *What Is* the *Alliance* for *National Renewal?* Denver: National Civic League, 1996; *Better Together: The Report of the Saguaro Seminar.* Cambridge, Mass.: Kennedy School of Government, Harvard University, Dec. 2000; and Delli Carpini, M. *The Youth Civic Engagement Initiative.* Philadelphia: Pew Charitable Trusts, Sept. 2000.

12. We focus on some of these in the concluding sections of chapters two through five of Sirianni and Friedland (2001).

13. The civic renewal movement does not seek to displace other movements for rights and justice, which perform many important functions that the civic renewal movement cannot directly perform. Many of the civic movements we have mentioned include issues of rights, recognition, power, and justice, as well as periodically using confrontational methods to gain a seat at the table. Indeed, many see themselves as located in multiple movements simultaneously. This complexity and multiple identification is not unusual in social movements.

14. In fact, all presentations could be digitally taped and made available for editing and use by July congress sponsors and participants, subject to copyright approval by the presenters and broadcast partners (such as a public television collaborative).

15. Each convening of the National Civic Congress would cost several million dollars. If each team of five or so delegates were subsidized at an average of $3,000 for travel and lodging and expected to raise the difference, three hundred teams could be brought to the July gathering for $900,000. Staff, convention center, and media project costs would be added to this number. A more ambitious media strategy would include interviews and taping in the home community and Web-based stories and case studies prior to each congress.

16. With increasing focus among an array of organizations and foundations on youth civic engagement, it might be possible to begin with a Youth Civic Congress in 2004, representing teams of young people and their adult partners from various organizational networks who are beginning to come together to strategize about how to build a broad youth civic engagement movement and how to use the presidential election season of 2004 to give visibility to it.

After we developed the original draft of this proposal for a National Civic Congress, a proposal for declaring an annual National Civic Participation Week was offered in the Senate by Dianne Feinstein and Pat Roberts. These proposals are quite different from ours; they could possibly be made to complement each other.

Carmen Sirianni is professor of sociology and public policy at Brandeis University.

Lewis A. Friedland is associate professor in the School of Journalism and Mass Communication at the University of Wisconsin–Madison. Friedland and Sirianni codirect the Youth Civic Engagement Project and the Civic Practices Network (www.cpn.org).

Unity and Community in the Twenty-First Century

Ted Halstead, Michael Lind

"Americans of all ages, all stations in life, and all types of disposition, are for-ever forming associations," the French philosopher Alexis de Tocqueville observed in his famous 1835 tract, *Democracy in America.* "There are not only commercial and industrial associations in which all take part, but others of a thousand different types—religious, moral, serious, futile, very general and very limited, immensely large and very minute. . . . Nothing, in my view, deserves more attention than the intellectual and moral associations in America."[1]

What Tocqueville described as "the intellectual and moral associations in America" constitute the third sector of U.S. society—the realm of community, or civil society. This third sector is far more complex and diverse than the eco-nomic and governmental sectors of our society. For instance, it includes an enormous variety of associations with differing goals and claims on the indi-vidual, ranging from globe-spanning religious institutions that comprise many smaller organizations to philanthropic foundations, charities of all kinds, and membership associations as undemanding as amateur softball teams and bird-watching clubs. At the same time, most Americans also share a broader sense of national community, reinforced by common customs, freedoms, and cul-tural narratives, and a common language. It is this broader sense of commu-nity that fosters national unity even as it gives force and meaning to the concepts of American citizenship.

Civil society in the United States has grown more inclusive over time. From the late eighteenth century to the early twenty-first century, our national community has evolved from one in which citizenship was limited to white Christian men of predominantly British descent into a highly diverse melting pot in which descendants of British colonial settlers are a minority among whites, and whites as a whole will be a national minority in a few generations.

Note: This article is adapted from *The Radical Center: The Future of American Politics,* by Ted Halstead and Michael Lind, copyright © 2001 by the authors. Used by permission of Doubleday, a division of Random House, Inc.

Equality in the community realm, however, has often lagged behind equality in the market and the state. Nonwhite Americans and women were granted at least nominal political and economic rights generations ago, even as they continued to be excluded from fashionable clubs, schools, and neighborhoods. As recently as the 1960s, elite social clubs that segregated on the basis of race and gender dominated the upper echelons of American community, and restrictive covenants in many neighborhoods prevented blacks and Jews—and sometimes Catholics—from moving in. Until the Supreme Court, in *Loving v. Virginia,* struck down antimiscegenation laws in 1967, roughly half the states banned marriage among U.S. citizens of different races, denying the right to exercise the most basic and intimate kind of voluntary association.

As these examples suggest, civil society can be a realm of exclusion and humiliation, as well as a realm of integration and personal fulfillment. Fundamental questions of civil rights have divided our nation since its very inception, giving rise to all-out civil war in the nineteenth century and a great deal of social unrest in the twentieth. The racial and ethnic bigotry that has resulted in mistreatment of various minority groups—our nation's perennial shame—represent the dark side of our community sector. The Ku Klux Klan and other vigilante groups enforcing the norms of the dominant local majority, and the Social Register attempting to create an American aristocracy, have been as much a part of the history of American community as the United Way and public libraries.

More typical, fortunately, has been the beneficial side of our communal institutions, be they secular or religious. In fact, it has often been voluntary institutions in the communal sphere that come to the rescue of our citizenry in times of great need. When the first wave of industrialization in the United States created massive social dislocation, our community sector responded by creating an array of caregiving institutions such as the Salvation Army and church-based missions. Other institutions such as the Boy Scouts and Girl Scouts helped assimilate an enormous population of immigrants and rural children to middle-class norms, while bowling and other amateur sports gave working-class and rural Americans new forms of recreation and interaction. The community sector came to the rescue again after World War II, when the internal combustion engine and electrification created the car-based suburb. To combat isolation and anomie, voluntary organizations created a flourishing suburban culture, characterized by Little League and more recently by soccer teams, as well as giant villagelike churches and synagogues.

The Community Sector in the Twenty-First Century

In considering the future of our community sector in the twenty-first century, then, two overarching questions rise to the surface: What forms will community institutions take in the century ahead? How inclusive will the community sector be as a whole?

The first question is almost impossible to answer, except after the fact. The Tocquevillian associations of American community, if they are genuine, are the product of spontaneous effort on the part of motivated individuals and groups, not the result of a master plan designed by visionary intellectuals and imposed from the top down by government officials. What is more, their sheer diversity, in both form and goal, is limited only by the boundaries of the law and the imagination. Among other factors, technological change can lead to unprecedented changes in the community sector, as it does in the market and the government. Before the invention of the television, nobody could have predicted the appearance of evangelists with a world reach; before the spread of the personal computer and the World Wide Web, nobody could have envisioned the proliferation of online virtual communities in the form of Internet chat rooms.

This suggests that when reformers propose policies intended to preserve and revitalize community in the United States, we must be skeptical. It is not that their concerns are not legitimate. Indeed, our sense of community is under attack on many fronts. For example, the segmenting effects of new technology and new media make it ever more difficult for Americans to feel that they share a common frame of reference. The speed and occupational mobility that are hallmarks of the digital age make it more difficult for people to know their neighbors and to identify with a particular geographic community. The number of Americans now living alone, as well as the number who express feelings of loneliness, is skyrocketing. Then too, institutions that once afforded a common bond, as with the military draft, have vanished and not been replaced. Even our sports stadiums are not what they used to be; many are now branded with corporate names, and separate entrances and private booths now cordon off the members of the elite overclass from the general public.

Naturally, these challenges to our community life and national cohesion lead elected officials and aspiring social reformers to propose community-enhancing cures of all kinds. For instance, we frequently hear the call for expanding or reinvigorating civil society. Embedded in many of these community-building plans, however, is a seldom-noticed contradiction: our ability to consciously promote a vibrant national community is extremely limited. Unlike the economic realm, which is organized primarily by markets and creative destruction, or the governmental realm, which is structured by rules of law and detailed policies, the communal realm is shaped by forces that cannot be easily identified or manipulated. Indeed, the fact that community is the realm most resistant to any model or scheme explains why so many well-intentioned plans for improving our nation's community life fail to achieve their intended result.

The problem is as much conceptual as practical. For centuries, philosophers have debated the legitimacy of various approaches to social change. Some, including the Marquis de Condorcet, Auguste Comte, Karl Marx, Jeremy Bentham, and other rationalist philosophers of the Enlightenment tradition, have sought to reform existing institutions in light of an abstract ideal or goal, by deducing first principles of social order. Pragmatists such as John Dewey and Richard Rorty have rejected grand master plans and called for ceaseless experimentation in designing institutions. Skeptical thinkers, such as David Hume, Edmund Burke, Isaiah Berlin, and John Gray, have criticized the notion that society can be redesigned by either abstract reason or pragmatic experimentation. Society, they have argued, is not a mechanical construction but an organic entity, based on gradually evolving traditions. The task of reformers is to water and fertilize—and, now and then, to prune—a growing plant.

This "Burkean" approach to society has significant limitations, particularly in the sectors of the economy and government, where the pressure of changing circumstances forces business organizations to rely on pragmatic planning and experimentation and obliges government officials to engage in rational reform, to the best of their ability. In the realm of community, however, suspicion of any grand attempt at social engineering and emphasis on the spontaneous generation of social order are much more justified. Indeed, political philosopher Francis Fukuyama has argued that although particular kinds of "social capital" are disrupted by technological and economic change, over time "the stock of social capital is constantly being replenished."[2] If one era's community institutions fade, then their purpose may be better served by new institutions, which may only now be emerging.

Since our community sector evolves organically instead of intentionally, the best policy for nurturing new voluntary institutions is often to let them adapt on their own, with minimal outside intervention. This is particularly the case in a country like the United States that has a long tradition of accomplishing by voluntary association much of what is done by government in other nations. Does this mean that those concerned about the well-being of our national community as a whole should do nothing? No. Rather, it means that the best way to strengthen our community sector may be through indirect methods such as removing or reducing the most serious social divisions in our community, while relying on the resilience, entrepreneurism, and good will of Americans to do the rest.

What, then, are the foremost threats to an inclusive and cohesive American national community in the decades to come? Perhaps the biggest question in the coming century is whether the United States will evolve into a highly integrated nation that shares a common identity and destiny, or into a mere collection of rival groups that share little more than a territory and a set of political institutions. At the beginning of the twenty-first century, the integrity of the American community is threatened by three great divides: the racial divide, the generational divide, and the genetic divide. The racial divide is the oldest and deepest in U.S. society. The generational divide is a recent phenomenon, caused by the burdens that the graying of the U.S. population will impose on the working-age public. The genetic divide is a social division that does not yet exist but might be created by the abuse of the rapidly developing technology of genetic engineering. (The class divide is another enduring problem in the United States, one that influences the three others. However, governmental and economic reforms are more salient in ameliorating this division than indirect community-oriented reforms are, so for the purposes of this article the class divide is not directly addressed.)

Each divide poses distinct dilemmas that require distinct solutions. Whether the United States thrives or fails in the twenty-first century will depend in large part on whether we as a people can prevent the racial, generational, and genetic divides from fissuring our hard-won and still fragile sense of an American community that transcends the smaller communities of ethnicity, class, religion, and region. If we can remove these fundamental roadblocks, we may be pleasantly surprised by just how well our community sector thrives in the decades ahead and brings out the very best in all Americans.

The Racial Divide

Let us begin with the oldest and most destructive divide in America's community, the racial. Although much progress has been made in recent decades toward tearing down racial boundaries and ensuring civil rights for all Americans, much still remains to be done. At the dawn of the Information Age, the American people must once again ask themselves whether they aspire to be a truly unified nation.

By the year 2000, California had become the first "postminority" state in the nation, meaning that whites no longer made up the majority of the state's population. By the year 2100, the nation as a whole may reach a similar majority-minority profile, in which the number of "whites" will be outnumbered by the total number of Americans of other races. For the most part, this will be the result of intermarriage and today's historically high level of immigration, which if maintained is projected to lead to a full doubling of the U.S. population by the end of the century.

Demography may be destiny, but it is a destiny that can be shaped and altered by choices—our choices. It is within our power as a nation to decide whether we are going to be an integrated nation of individuals with different ancestries, or a balkanized multinational state in which the government assigns every citizen to this or that arbitrarily defined racial category, favoring some while discriminating against others. It is also within our power as a nation to decide, by way of our immigration policies, both the general size of our future population and the relative mix between high-skilled and low-skilled populations and workforces. Over the long run, this may be the most important choice of all.

We believe that reforms in the realm of community should be citizen-based. Our ultimate goal is to help foster an ever-evolving but ever-more-integrated nation, in which common citizenship and common democratic values outweigh racial and other divisions. When it comes to civil rights, we argue for a combination of color-blind public policies and strong antidiscrimination laws, which combination in our opinion offers the best hope for integrating our remarkably diverse population into a dynamic yet cohesive whole. With regard to immigration, we advocate a policy geared to the nature and demands of an information age, on the basis of a more even balance between high-skilled and low-skilled immigrants. These policies would help not only to unite our nation but also to restore the original vision of America's greatest civil rights leaders.

Following the abolition of formal racial segregation in the mid-1960s, civil rights reformers disagreed about the next stage. Some, such as Martin Luther King, Jr., and Bayard Rustin, favored abolishing racial labels based on biological origins altogether, and pursuing race-neutral approaches to combating poverty among all races. In 1963, for instance, King proposed including poor white citizens among the beneficiaries of a Bill of Rights for the Disadvantaged: "It is a simple matter of justice that America, in dealing creatively with the task of raising the Negro from backwardness, should also be rescuing a large stratum of the forgotten white poor."[3]

This race-neutral, need-based approach lost out, by the 1970s, to a race-based, need-neutral approach to civil rights. The emphasis of public policy shifted from antipoverty programs that helped all disadvantaged Americans to affirmative action or racial preferences that benefited affluent as well as poor members of racial minorities, while excluding disadvantaged whites. To build political support for these new group-based preferences, liberals in the 1960s and 1970s extended preferences to Latin American immigrants and women. Broadening the scope of affirmative action in this way won political allies for the program, at the price of destroying its moral legitimacy. Today a majority of the beneficiaries of affirmative action—a program originally intended to help the descendants of American slaves—are middle-class white women and voluntary immigrants from Latin America and their children who arrived in this country after the civil rights revolution in the 1960s and cannot claim to have suffered under the pre-1960s forms of institutionalized racism. Inevitably, this incoherent regime of selective preferences created a backlash. In the past decade, the preference system has been trimmed back by federal courts as well as state governments. There is now a growing consensus that the race-conscious policies of the past thirty years have polarized the American people, without significantly reducing socioeconomic disparities among U.S. racial and ethnic groups.

Moreover, a high level of racial intermarriage and recent genetic discoveries are rapidly rendering our system of racial classification obsolete. Newly arrived immigrants from Latin America and East Asia are intermarrying with the post-European white majority at a remarkable rate—one in two Asian Americans, one in three Latinos. The younger Americans are, the more likely they are to be in a transracial marriage. In 1990, for example, only 53 percent of married black Americans under the age of twenty-five were in black-black marriages, compared to 84 percent of blacks over the age of sixty-five.[4] Nothing short of a complete reversal of today's high intermarriage rate can prevent the formation, at rates varying with the region of the country, of a mixed-race majority in the United States by 2100. Golfer Tiger Woods—who jokingly describes himself as "Cablinasian," by which he means a fusion of Caucasian, Black, Indian, and Asian—may well be a forerunner of the "average American" in the centuries to come.

As that example suggests, our arbitrary system of racial labels is collapsing under the weight of its own absurdity and complexity. Federal government assignment of American citizens to this or that "race" should come to an end. Subnational ethnic and racial identities should be a matter of voluntary affiliation, neither encouraged nor discouraged by law. In the twenty-first century, American citizens, whether native or naturalized, should be classified by the government as members of only one nation—the United States—and only one race—the human race.

Abolition of racial labels should be accompanied by abolition of race-based public policy. As early as 1871, Frederick Douglass, the abolitionist who had escaped from slavery, dismissed the radical black nationalist Martin Delany's call for racial quotas as "absurd." Douglass wrote: "According to the census, the colored people of the country constitute one-eighth of the whole American people. Upon your statistical principle, the colored people of the United States ought, therefore, not only to hold one-eighth of all offices in the country, but they should own one-eighth of all the property, and pay one-eighth of all the taxes of the country. . . . Now, my old friend, there is no man in the United States who knows better than you do that equality of numbers has nothing to do with equality of attainments."[5] As an alternative to feel-good tokenism, Douglass favored bringing about genuine equality of attainment between black and white Americans by means of social reform.

The legitimate goals of affirmative action, such as increasing the presence of blacks and Latinos in higher education, the professions, and politics, can and should be pursued—but by such race-neutral methods as better primary education for all Americans. In his classic autobiography *Hunger of Memory,* Richard Rodriguez pointed out the essential flaw of affirmative action as a tool of social mobility: "Those least disadvantaged were helped first, advanced because many others of their race were more disadvantaged. The strategy of affirmative action, finally, did not take seriously the educational dilemma of disadvantaged students. They need good early schooling!"[6] Measures to combat racial separation by class and subculture, such as equalization of school funding, would also help lower-class whites, who remain a majority of the nation's poor.

The era of preferences for favored groups and penalties for disfavored groups should be replaced by a new era of identical individual rights for all Americans. To prevent racist sentiments that do exist from being translated into action, antidiscrimination laws should remain in place, to help all victims of racial discrimination, nonwhite and white alike.

In the twenty-first century, the United States has the potential not only to live up to Douglass's and King's original visions of a color blind nation but also to become the most racially mixed and integrated nation in the developed world. For this to happen, we need to abandon the system of racial classifications and preferences that, at this stage in our nation's history, only serves to reinforce racial differences instead of diminishing them, and to polarize our nation instead of unifying it.

Discussing the downside and unintended consequences of our current system of racial preferences is controversial. But there may be no topic more difficult to discuss in our country today than our immigration policy—so wedded are many Americans to predetermined views on both sides of this issue, and so quick are they to accuse their detractors of malevolent intentions. Yet when it comes to the long-term profile and health of the American nation—meaning, the very size of our population, our educational and economic makeup, and our race relations—no other factor may be as important. Indeed, immigration is by far the largest source of U.S. population growth, and if today's historically high rate of immigration continues, our total population will more than double by the end of the century.

The reason the immigration debate is so contentious is that any policy choice inevitably involves significant trade-offs. There is simply no such thing as a win-win immigration policy; whatever choice is made, there will always be winners and losers, both domestically and internationally. For instance, a high level of low-skilled immigration (most of the current immigrants to the United States fall in this category) tends to benefit domestic employers and capital owners, as well as the poor from abroad who come to our shores. However, the same policy also tends to depress wages for America's current working poor, and to increase the disparity between our educational and economic haves and have-nots. In studying this matter, the National Academy of Sciences concluded that increased immigration tends to disproportionately depress the wages and economic circumstances of low-skilled and low-income workers, while benefiting the wealthiest Americans. Immigration is now the chief factor contributing to the growth of poverty in the United States. Between 1979 and 1997, for instance, as much as 75 percent of the increase in the size of the total American poor population resulted from immigration. According to the Urban Institute, an increase of 10 percent in immigration reduces the wages of the immigrants already here by as much as 9 percent.[7]

Our collective challenge is to forge an immigration policy that reflects our nation's perennial values and long-term objectives while balancing the interests of various sectors of our society. There is no question that the preeminent position of the United States in the world today owes a great deal to our embrace of newcomers from around the globe. What is more, the fact that the fertility rate of native-born Americans is below the replacement level may mean that some amount of immigration is necessary to prevent the U.S. population from shrinking. For several reasons, then, we believe that for the foreseeable future the United States should continue to welcome at least some immigrants into our community. The big questions, however, are where and how to draw the line, and what the relative mix between low-skilled and high-skilled immigrants should be.

The most obvious starting point is to rethink the present mix of skilled and unskilled immigrants. Because of an emphasis on family reunification, 65–70 percent of visas are now allotted to family members of U.S. citizens and lawful permanent residents, many of whom are poor and uneducated. In 1996, fully 35.8 percent of immigrants had less than a high school education; by comparison, only 9.7 percent of U.S.-born citizens lacked a high school diploma. Today Canada, with a system that awards points to skilled immigrants, brings in people with better qualifications from the same countries that send the United States their unskilled workers.

In a knowledge-based economy, when the educational attainments of our citizenry are among the most important determinants of our nation's economic success, a policy of flooding the U.S. labor market with uneducated workers is simply self-defeating. An immigration policy geared to Information Age America would favor skilled immigrants over unskilled immigrants. Throughout its history, the United States has benefited from the talents of immigrant scientists such as Albert Einstein; immigrant inventors the likes of Alexander Graham Bell, Guglielmo Marconi, and An Wang; and immigrant businessmen, Andrew Carnegie for one. In the twenty-first century, we should build on this tradition by tipping the balance in favor of educated and enterprising newcomers from other lands.

Limiting family-based immigration to spouses, minor children, and parents of citizens and lawful permanent residents—a reform suggested by the U.S. Commission on Immigration Reform headed by the late Barbara Jordan—would greatly reduce the proportion of unskilled to skilled immigrants. An immigration policy that favors skilled immigrants would reduce the immigrant-caused growth of poverty in the United States. At the same time, a skill-based immigration policy would reduce the rate of U.S. population growth. Economically successful people of all races tend to have a fertility rate at or below replacement.

Needless to say, too heavy a reliance on well-educated foreign workers to fill our domestic jobs could backfire by reducing the incentives to improve our own schools and universities, or to upgrade the skills of our current population. To reduce this risk and ensure that U.S. citizens as well as recent immigrants remain first in line for new jobs in the future, it may well be advisable to gradually lower our overall level of immigration from today's historic highs while encouraging more Americans to choose careers based on math and science. (Between 1986 and 1996, the percentage of bachelor's degrees conferred in the United States in natural sciences, health sciences, and computer science and engineering actually declined from 28.2 percent to 24.0 percent.)

Of course, there are some labor-intensive occupations—particularly in caregiving fields such as nursing—that do not require highly educated workers. As our society ages, there may come a time when once again we need to increase the number of unskilled immigrants to satisfy the demand for such jobs. For the foreseeable future, however, a policy that raises our proportion of skilled immigrants and gradually lowers our overall immigration level would not only boost our competitiveness, productivity, and living standards; it would disproportionately help the poorest American workers of all races, the ones who suffer the most as a result of today's irrational and outdated immigration regimen. In fact, the new approaches to civil rights and immigration that we propose would reinforce one another and do far more to help all of the neediest Americans get ahead, while promoting rather than retarding racial integration in the process.

The Generational Divide

The racial divide represents the oldest fissure in the American national community; the generational divide is the most recent. By *generational divide* we mean political conflict among Americans on a generational basis. This is not a new phenomenon in our politics, but it will be elevated to new heights in the decades ahead.

The late twentieth century in the United States saw the emergence for the first time of the elderly as a special-interest group. The American Association of Retired Persons (AARP) became one of the most powerful lobbies in U.S. politics. Special-interest politics of the elderly is the unwelcome result of a welcome development: the increasing health and longevity of our population.

Within a few years, for the first time in our nation's history, there will be fewer Americans aged twenty to twenty-nine than people fifty-five to sixty-nine. By 2020, the younger group may shrink to 40 percent smaller than the older group. The Census Bureau predicts that the elderly—whose numbers were roughly equal to those of eighteen to twenty-one-year-olds in 1940—will outnumber college-age Americans by almost four to one in 2040. Between 1950 and 1992, the life expectancy for white men at age sixty-five rose by 21 percent; for white women, by 25 percent. Thanks to this increased longevity, by the 1990s more than 40 percent of Americans between fifty and fifty-nine had living family members from four or more generations. Indeed, the number of Americans now living beyond the age of one hundred has mushroomed; there are seventy thousand centenarians in this country. Advances in genetic therapy and biomedical research will only extend the average life span in the future.[8]

The fact that U.S. citizens are enjoying a longer life should be cause for celebration. Unfortunately, several factors cloud what ought to be a joyous development: the competition for resources between the growing number of elderly citizens and the shrinking number of young Americans; the coming crisis of caregiving that will manifest itself when the members of the baby boom generation reach their final years; and a much-neglected but equally important phenomenon, the spatial and geographic segregation of Americans by age. All three of these trends are exacerbated by the new reality of generational voting blocks, more specifically by the fact that today's elderly tend to vote in high numbers, while the young tend to do just the opposite (for which the young have only themselves to blame.) Unless these potential problems are redressed relatively soon, the promise of an aging United States may turn very sour.

The most frequently discussed source of intergenerational strife stems from the interaction between our changing demographic profile and the design of our social welfare programs for retirees. When Social Security was introduced by Franklin Roosevelt, the initial number of recipients was too small to be politically significant. But medical advances and the declining birthrate have combined to change all of that. As mentioned, the latest projections are that our Social Security system will start paying out more than it takes in as of 2016—and become insolvent as of 2038.[9] The prognosis is even more alarming for Medicare, the other main entitlement program for retirees.

These fiscal problems have, of course, been compounded by the political problem that the elderly tend to vote en masse—for politicians who promise to defend and increase their retirement and health care benefits. One result is that the rate of growth of entitlements for the elderly is outstripping the rate of growth of the economy as a whole. Because the size of government in relation to the economy is unlikely to expand, additional growth in spending on the elderly has to come at the expense of spending on other social needs, notably child care and education. Overspending on one generation of retirees could therefore lead to dramatic underspending on the generations that follow, which would compromise our collective future.

Although there has been much public debate about the coming strains on our Social Security and Medicare systems, there has been relatively little debate about the broader caregiving crisis to come. Advances in medicine may well permit the elderly to live and work longer, and to be healthier at later stages in life; but the same advances are likely to prolong the period in which they need time-consuming and expensive care.

Between 1987 and 1996, the number of nursing homes increased by 20 percent. Roughly half of the cost of long-term care is paid for by patients and their families; at an average cost of $40,000 per year, nursing home care is quite expensive. The financial cost of caring for the elderly is joined by the cost in time and effort. Already by 1997, 22 percent of U.S. families were providing care for an elderly relative. According to one estimate, the value of the care provided by family caregivers amounts to an annual total of $196 billion—compared to the $73 billion a year spent by government on long-term care.[10] Needless to say, these pressures will increase dramatically as a result of the graying of the baby boom generation.

The need to provide unprecedented individualized care for the elderly, especially for nonfamily members, can be expected to deepen the tension between working-age citizens and retired citizens. Young parents struggling to raise their own children, and perhaps to care for their own parents or grandparents, will resent the demand of single-issue lobbies representing the elderly for more government resources for eldercare. For their part, the elderly will feel that they have earned a right to a high standard of care by their contributions to society during their working lives. Each cohort will naturally be tempted to look out for its own interests—which, sadly, will be in diametric opposition to one another.

Finally, the emerging generational divide is widened further by our bizarre system of residential segregation by age. In today's United States, one neighborhood may consist predominantly of young working families, while another is inhabited almost exclusively by retirees. There are even entire states—Florida and Arizona come quickly to mind—dominated by retirees. This age apartheid encourages irrational political behavior on the part of retirees, demanding that unseen working-age people somewhere else support them, as well as with working adults, who rebel against supporting old people with whom they have no sense of connection. It also encourages geographically concentrated age groups to vote against the interests of the generational minorities in their own vicinity; for example, elderly voting blocks typically oppose new local spending initiatives for public education. Obviously, if the young and old lived among one another, there would be a greater inclination to realize that a community involves trade-offs and cooperation across generations.

What can be done about the generational divide? Fortunately, a great deal. We have to remember that the generational divide is not the result of bad motives on the part of elderly or nonelderly voters. It is simply another case where the rational pursuit of self-interest by many individuals, without any coordination, results in collective problems. The answer, then, lies in changing the norms, incentives, and barriers that cause today's generational divide, to permit a healthier and more complementary relationship among all generations to emerge.

The most important remedy may be wholesale rethinking of the process of retirement. If individuals routinely live into their nineties and even hundreds, why should we maintain social, employment, and legal conventions suggesting that the individual should cease to be a productive member of the workforce for the final twenty-five to thirty-five years of life? We have everything to gain from encouraging all U.S. citizens to remain healthy and productive members of society for as long as they can. Given the option, many Americans may well choose to remain in the workforce into their seventies, if not eighties.

Alternatively, many Americans may choose to devote their later years to giving back to society in a variety of ways, by caring for the very young, the very needy, or the very old. Indeed, retirees could well turn into the new army of volunteers that our community sector so needs. The *Journal of Gerontology* reported in 1999 that Americans over age sixty-five who volunteered a minimum of forty hours a year were a full 67 percent more likely to live longer than their counterparts who did not.[11] But for this virtuous cycle to replace today's vicious cycle, we must eliminate our fixed retirement age and enable America's septuagenarians, octogenarians, and even nonagenarians to remain in the workforce for as long as they choose, or to take up a new vocation as part of America's armies of compassion.

If one way to lessen the entitlement burden that is widening the generational divide is to do away with a fixed retirement age, then the second is to reinvent our entire approach to social welfare. The United States needs a new social contract for the twenty-first century, one that is not based on employers or intergenerational transfers, but rather on individual citizens. By increasing the degree to which pensions and health care are paid for by compulsory savings, of the kind proposed in various plans for partial privatization of Social Security, rather than almost exclusively on transfer payments from today's workers to today's retirees, we could solve the very design problem that turns demographic variance between generations into a fiscal time bomb for all involved. It is not a moment too soon to begin moving from our Industrial Age social contract to an Information Age one. Indeed, it is difficult to imagine a policy change that would do more to bring about long-term political peace and equity between generations.

Another major barrier standing in the way of intergenerational harmony is physical, resulting from outmoded zoning laws. A typical American may grow up in a middle-class suburb and spend the college years in an "apartment city" surrounded by tens of thousands of single young people, before spending the rest of the life cycle in a neighborhood for young couples with "starter" homes, a more prosperous middle-class neighborhood for families with children, and finally a neighborhood where everyone is old. The New Urbanism movement advocates mixed-use land policies in constructing new suburbs and revitalizing urban cores to create neighborhoods in which people of all ages and various income groups live among each other and mingle daily. Except in "greenfield" developments, realizing this ideal requires substantial revision of zoning laws—for example, by allowing families to build "granny flats" adjacent to their homes, which can also be used by young people in college or low-income workers. Needless to say, the opportunities for the elderly to contribute to community can only be maximized if they reside among younger neighbors, instead of being warehoused among hundreds or thousands of other old people.

Changing our nation's retirement norms, our basic social contract, and our residential zoning laws could do a great deal to alleviate what is fast becoming a festering generational divide in our political and community spheres. But no matter how successful such policies are, how integrated our generations become, and how long our senior citizens remain healthy and productive members of society, there would still be one big challenge left unaddressed: how to care for the growing number of senior citizens in their final years. Americans in the twenty-first century will have obligations to a growing number of living parents and grandparents (and great-grandparents, and perhaps even great-great-grandparents).

Providing America's shrinking families with the help they need for their growing number of elderly members is a joint responsibility of the state and the community. If the burden falls primarily on the state, however, it only exacerbates the fiscal burdens and political tensions already caused by our aging society. Fortunately, there is an alternative that is particularly suited to the U.S. context. Throughout our history, we Americans have looked to charities and volunteerism to perform many of the tasks that are taken on in other societies by a paternalistic government. It may be, then, that such American philanthropic institutions as charities, foundations, and churches can once again come to the rescue of the broader society, this time meeting at least part of the unprecedented need for provision of quality eldercare in the coming century.

Is it realistic to expect the nonprofit sector—staffed, in part, by healthy retirees—to play a significant role in caring for the needy elderly? One of America's most unique and heartening virtues is the strong philanthropic impulse of our citizens. Indeed, Americans donate far more money to charities—both per capita and overall—than any other nation on the planet. In 1999, for instance, approximately 70 percent of our citizenry donated to charities of some sort. The combined total in charitable giving in that year was $190 billion, of which approximately 75 percent came from individuals, 10 percent from foundations, 8 percent from bequests, and 6 percent from corporations.[12]

The strong American tradition of voluntarism is as encouraging as our tradition of charitable giving. In 1999, for instance, 49 percent of Americans reported that they volunteered for a community purpose, compared to only 19 percent of citizens of France and 13 percent in Germany.[13] There is reason to hope that the level of volunteerism can increase further in the coming decades, particularly if the large number of relatively healthy senior citizens decide to enter the voluntary sector en masse.

Of course, this requires not just a new army of volunteers but also a significant expansion of charitable funding. Fortunately for our nation as whole—and potentially for our neediest citizens—we can expect a generational wealth transfer of enormous proportions over the next half-century, a significant portion of which will go to charitable causes. Researchers John Havens and Paul Schervich predict a total wealth transfer of between $41 trillion and $136 trillion over the next fifty-five years. By 2025, it is estimated that charitable giving alone could surpass $1.2 trillion per year (in inflation adjusted dollars).[14] To put this figure in context, this is nearly twice as much money as our government currently spends on all domestic discretionary programs. As this example suggests, America's philanthropic largesse could go a long way toward alleviating the coming crisis of eldercare as well as many other social problems—assuming, that is, that this level of giving materializes, and that a significant portion is directed toward helping the neediest and oldest Americans.

The charitable tax deduction, first enacted in 1917, has played a significant role in encouraging philanthropy, by rewarding the contributor with a tax break in direct proportion to generosity (although such deductions accrue only to those who itemize on their tax form). Unfortunately, the nonprofit sector as it exists today in the United States is not particularly well positioned to play a greater role in relieving the burden of care for the elderly that would otherwise fall on the government. First, relatively few of today's growing number of nonprofit and community organizations are of a strictly caregiving nature. Second, many of the branches of civil society that are thriving today (with the possible exception of certain religious denominations) are of an elite nature. At the turn of the twenty-first century, elite-oriented charitable organizations—the opera, private universities, environmental groups, and soccer leagues—are thriving. But many of the communities and constituencies most in need—particularly the young, the old, and the inner-city poor—are not receiving the resources they need.

Currently, approximately 43 percent of philanthropic contributions flow to religious institutions, 14 percent to educational institutions (mostly higher education), 9 percent to health, 9 percent to human services, 6 percent to arts and culture, and 3 percent to environmental causes.[15] Clearly, the majority of philanthropic dollars do not go into direct services for the neediest Americans.

Could a larger share of philanthropic dollars be redirected toward relieving the strain on families in the area of care giving, without undermining the philanthropic impulse or freedom of choice of individual donors? The United States now recognizes two broad types of nonprofit institution: those focusing on lobbying and those that are primarily charitable in nature. Contributions to the former are not tax deductible, while contributions to the latter are. We propose expanding this binary system into a trinary system, by distinguishing between two types of tax-exempt organization: the minority (the Salvation Army, a church soup kitchen) entirely dedicated to providing direct care to the neediest, and the majority (most religious institutions, universities, membership organizations, the opera) serving the public interest, but not as directly. In our opinion, the strictly caregiving organizations should receive even more favorable tax treatment, to reflect their greater importance to the well-being of our society as a whole. Accordingly, we propose that donations to this new type of caregiving organization be rewarded through tax deductions worth 150 percent of the value of the contribution (as opposed to the consistent rate of 100 percent for all other charities).

Naturally, new regulations need to be enacted to ensure that the charities benefiting from this special deduction are devoted solely to caregiving for the neediest populations, and to prevent both donors and nonprofit organizations from gaming the system.

Such a policy, if it proved effective in steering a larger portion of charitable gifts toward direct service for the neediest, could become one of the most innovative and important means of addressing the crises of senior care that we will face in the coming decades, while at the same time helping the chronically poor of all ages, many of whom risk being left behind in the new economy. Given the amount of likely philanthropic giving in coming years, the results could be dramatic. Many Americans would choose to connect their own philanthropic and economic interests with those of the neediest citizens, and the new wave of funding could inspire a whole new array of caregiving organizations. In fact, many of today's religious and secular nonprofit organizations would likely create a caregiving offshoot of their own to take advantage of the preferential tax treatment, while allocating more of their resources to alleviating human suffering of multiple types. Ideally, a whole new spirit of entrepreneurship, volunteerism, and innovation would arise in the caregiving sector. Along with the other reforms we propose, this might help turn what is now shaping up to be a vicious generational divide into a virtuous intergenerational collaboration.

The Genetic Divide

If the racial divide is a threat to American community inherited from the past, and the generational divide is a threat of the present, the genetic divide may be the greatest threat to community in the future. By *genetic divide,* we mean the prospect that in the future it may be possible for people to upgrade the genes of their offspring and create a profound division between the majority of ordinary citizens and a minority of genetically superior individuals.

By 2001, there were already 450 genetic tests in the research development pipeline, paving the way for a whole new wave of medications custom tailored to a patient's genetic profile. Next will come genetic therapy, the practice by which the genetic disposition of a living human being is altered to cure various gene-based illnesses. Then may come the day that replacement organs are routinely grown in vitro.

For all the novelty of these developments, however, the real turning point will come with the advent of germline modification. The basic difference between germline modification and other types of genetic therapy is that in the former the modification is passed on to future generations.

The debate over whether or how the ability to accomplish this should be permitted or regulated is unlikely to fall along conventional liberal-conservative lines. The view that such modification should be prohibited is likely to have adherents among people on the political left and right. The prohibitionist wing of the left is represented today by those American and European liberals who are opposed to the use of genetic engineering in farming. This faction on the left can be expected to oppose even the most benign forms of germline engineering as a fundamental misuse of technology. The antigenetics left will find allies among fundamentalist Christians, Jews, and Muslims, who believe that it is blasphemous for human beings to "play God" by altering the basic genomes of humans or other organisms.

The view that germline modification should be permitted is likely to find supporters among progressives who don't have such qualms about using advances in sophisticated technologies to improve the human condition and among right-wing libertarians who, unlike religious conservatives, celebrate economic dynamism and scientific progress. Whether they are on the left, right, or center of the political spectrum, these "legalizers" agree that the potential of germline modification to improve human health should be cautiously explored.

In making their case to outlaw all germline modification, the prohibitionists can cite the damage done by eugenics enthusiasts in the early twentieth century. Long before association with genocidal Nazi policies tainted it, eugenics was favored by many progressives in the United States and Britain, among them Theodore Roosevelt, Oliver Wendell Holmes, H. G. Wells, and George Bernard Shaw. Unfazed by their ignorance of the mechanisms of hereditary, state governments in the United States in the first half of the twentieth century sterilized not only thousands of "idiots" who suffered from only slight mental retardation but also many ordinary people who were victimized because of their racial ancestry or their poverty. This kind of abuse of eugenics by authorities blinded by social prejudice, prohibitionists argue, could happen again.

This is an argument that deserves to be taken seriously. But practically every institution in U.S. society has been abused, at one time or another, in the service of caste or class. The potential for abuse is an argument for *regulation*, not for prohibition. In any event, it is doubtful that anyone in the twenty-first century United States would favor reviving the horrifying practice of compulsory sterilization of the allegedly unfit, or anything that might remotely resemble racial or class genocide. Those who did would be marginalized and dismissed by mainstream proponents of reasonable genetic intervention as well as by its adversaries.

The likely alternative to prohibition is legalization and regulation of certain forms of germline intervention. When it comes to providing a regulatory framework for such procedures, the legalizer school can be expected to divide into two groups according to whether they support germline enhancement in addition to germline therapy. Germline therapy can be defined as genetic elimination of undesirable traits. Germline enhancement, by contrast, is genetic addition of desirable traits.

Human germline therapy, if it becomes practicable, is likely to be the least controversial form of germline intervention. Indeed, few would oppose elimination or modification of genes that cause severe mental retardation, deformity, blindness and deafness, and chronic crippling illness. The argument that many severely retarded and handicapped people are able to lead decent lives is not an argument against eliminating the genetic origin of their afflictions. The fact that individual lepers were able to lead adequate and decent lives in some cases was not an argument against eliminating leprosy. Leper colonies are a thing of the past. Some day, schools for the blind and deaf and mentally retarded and congenitally insane may be unknown as well.

We think germline therapy should be permitted, if it becomes practical and safe, and we believe its scope should be strictly limited. Once we go beyond the area of gross mental and physical handicaps into the more complex area of temperament, the danger of social prejudice grows (as the era of state-sponsored sterilization in the United States proved). Societies, and classes and subcultures within the same society, assess "normal" behavior differently.

We simply do not know enough about the link between the personality traits we value and those we dislike to safely eliminate the latter. A population wired to be perky, industrious extroverts might also be a population bereft of certain kinds of intellectual creativity. Therapeutic germline modification, then, should be limited to the most extreme mental and physical handicaps. Tampering with the genes that influence temperament should be forbidden, at least until much more is known about the biological basis of personality and achievement.

Let us begin summing up our tentative conclusions, while noting that these are general principles to guide the public debate on these matters in the decades ahead, rather than specific policy proposals, which would indeed be premature at this stage.

We have argued from a technology-friendly egalitarian perspective for rules governing the emerging field of human genomics. If it becomes practicable and safe, then germline therapy should be legalized—but only on two conditions. First, it should be limited to eradicating only the grossest kinds of mental and physical defects, preferably by methods that do not require abortion. Second, this minimal version of germline intervention should be accessible to all citizens on the basis of need, rather than of wealth.

Germline intervention for enhancement purposes, by contrast, should be prohibited altogether. Even a universal program of germline enhancement might result in disaster, because of the folly of misguided parents or ignorant public authorities. More important, the danger that a political or economic elite might use such technology in an attempt to turn their descendants into a new species of humankind for selfish purposes makes it imperative to prohibit germline enhancement for the foreseeable future.

The very nature of the Information Age argues for a broadening of individual choices, in voting, education, retirement, employment, lifestyle, and racial identification. We also believe that women deserve the right to make their own reproductive choices, in the context of legal contraception and abortion, preferably in an early stage. At the same time, however, certain types of reproductive choice—such as the ability of parents to engineer designer babies through germline engineering–should be limited. In making this distinction, we are guided by the conviction that the well-being and unity of our nation must always supersede the individual rights of its citizens, in such cases where they come into direct conflict. In this scenario, unregulated use of this technology could undermine the egalitarian ethos that underlies the principles of our democracy and the promise of the American dream.

Conclusion

If the United States musters the will and the foresight to prevent the racial, generational, and genetic divides from tearing it apart, then the future of our community sector will be bright. In fact, the United States would have a great deal to be proud of. Not only would we have the most dynamic economy and strongest military in the world, but we would also have the most integrated and diverse population of any modern nation. Just as America set an example to the world of the twentieth century through its commitment to democracy, it could set an equally powerful example in the twenty-first century as the most integrated melting-pot nation on the globe, unified across racial, class, and generational lines.

This accomplishment would be so great that it could—and should—give rise to a renewed American sense of patriotism. A purely sentimental patriotism degenerates all too easily into xenophobia and jingoism; a purely intellectual patriotism is too weak to preserve a sense of community. What is needed is a critical patriotism, a patriotism of both the heart and the head. Such an approach can find an example in a famous toast by Stephen Decatur at Norfolk, Virginia, in 1816: "Our country! . . . may she always be in the right; but our country, right or wrong."[16] Carl Schurz, the great immigrant German American senator, improved on this in Chicago on October 17, 1899: "Our country, right or wrong. When right, to be kept right; when wrong, to be put right."[17]

Notes

1. De Tocqueville, A. *Democracy in America.* (J. P. Maier, ed., G. Lawrence, trans.) Garden City, N.Y.: Anchor, 1969, pp. 513-517.

2. Fukuyama, F. *The Great Disruption: Human Nature and the Reconstruction of Social Order.* New York: Free Press, 1999, p. 282.

3. King, M. L., Jr. *Why We Can't Wait.* New York: Harper and Row, 1963, p. 142.

4. See Holmes, S. A. "The Politics of Race and the Census." *New York Times,* Mar. 19, 2000, p. D3; Etzioni, A. "The Monochrome Society." *Public Interest,* no. 137 (fall 1999), p. 53; and Lind, M. "The Beige and the Black." *New York Times Magazine,* Aug. 16, 1998, p. 38.

5. Quoted in Levine, R. S. *Martin Delany, Frederick Douglass, and the Politics of Representative Identity.* Chapel Hill: University of North Carolina Press, 1997, p. 232.

6. Rodriguez, R. *Hunger of Memory: The Education of Richard Rodriguez.* New York: Bantam, 1982, p. 151.

7. "Annual Projections of the Total Resident Population as of July 1: Middle, Lowest, Highest, and Zero International Migration Series, 1999 to 2100." Washington, D.C.: Population Projections Branch, Population Division, U.S. Census Bureau, Nov. 2, 2000.

8. "Employment's New Age." (Editorial.) *New York Times,* July 30, 2000.

9. Palmer, J. L., and Saving, T. R. *Status of the Social Security and Medicare Programs: A Summary of 2001 Annual Report.* Washington, D.C.: Social Security and Medicare Board of Trustees, Mar. 2001.

10. "The Changing American Family." In *Economic Report of the President.* Washington, D.C.: Government Printing Office, 2000.

11. Cited in Bowman, L., and Howard, S. "Volunteering Enhances Longevity, Study Says." *Plain Dealer,* Mar. 4, 1999, A9.

12. "1999 Contributions: $190.16 Billion by Source of Contribution." Giving USA/AAFRC Trust for Philanthropy, www.aafrc.org/CHAR.HTM.

13. Greenfield, K. T. "A New Way of Giving." *Time,* July 24, 2000, p. 48.

14. Havens, J. J., and Schervish, P. G. "Millionaires and the Millennium: New Estimates of the Forthcoming Wealth Transfer and the Prospects for a Golden Age of Philanthropy." Report published by Social Welfare Research Institute of Boston College, Oct. 19, 1999.

15. "1999 Contributions: $190.16 Billion by Type of Recipient Organization." Giving USA 2000/AAFRC Trust for Philanthropy, www.aafrc.org.

16. Brady, C. T. *Stephen Decatur.* Boston: Small, Maynard, 1900.

17. Trefousse, H. L. *Carl Schurz, a Biography.* Knoxville: University of Tennessee Press, 1982.

Ted Halstead is president of the New America Foundation.

Michael Lind is a senior scholar at the New America Foundation.

ORDERING INFORMATION

MAIL ORDERS TO:
  Jossey-Bass
  989 Market Street
  San Francisco, CA 94103-1741

PHONE subscription or single-copy orders toll-free to (888) 378-2537 or to (415) 433-1767 (toll call).

FAX orders toll-free to (800) 481-2665.

SUBSCRIPTIONS cost $55.00 for individuals U.S./Canada/Mexico; $105.00 for U.S. institutions, agencies, and libraries; $145.00 for Canada institutions; $179.00 for international institutions. Standing orders are accepted. (For subscriptions outside the United States, orders must be prepaid in U.S. dollars by check drawn on a U.S. bank or charged to VISA, MasterCard, American Express, or Discover.)

SINGLE COPIES cost $23.00 plus shipping (see below) when payment accompanies order. Please include appropriate sales tax. Canadian residents, add GST and any local taxes. Billed orders will be charged shipping and handling. No billed shipments to Post Office boxes. (Orders from outside the United States must be prepaid in U.S. dollars drawn on a U.S. bank or charged to VISA, MasterCard, or American Express.)

Prices are subject to change without notice.

SHIPPING (single copies only): $30.00 and under, add $5.50; $30.01 to $50.00, add $6.50; $50.01 to $75.00, add $8.00; $75.01 to $100.00, add $10.00; $100.01 to $150.00, add $12.00. Call for information on overnight delivery or shipments outside the United States.

ALL ORDERS must include either the name of an individual or an official purchase order number. Please submit your orders as follows:
  Subscriptions: specify issue (for example, NCR 86:1) you would like subscription to begin with.
  Single copies: specify volume and issue number. Available from Volume 86 onward. For earlier issues, see below.

MICROFILM available from University Microfilms, 300 North Zeeb Road, Ann Arbor, MI 48106. Back issues through Volume 85 and bound volumes available from William S. Hein & Co., 1285 Main Street, Buffalo, NY 14209. Full text available in the electronic versions of the Social Sciences Index, H. W. Wilson Co., 950 University Avenue, Bronx, NY 10452, and in CD-ROM from EBSCO Publishing, 83 Pine Street, P.O. Box 2250, Peabody, MA 01960. The full text of individual articles is available via fax modem through Uncover Company, 3801 East Florida Avenue, Suite 200, Denver, CO 80210. For bulk reprints (50 or more), call David Famiano, Jossey-Bass, at (415) 433-1740.

DISCOUNTS FOR QUANTITY ORDERS are available. For information, please write to Jossey-Bass, 989 Market Street, San Francisco, CA 94103-1741.

LIBRARIANS are encouraged to write to Jossey-Bass for a free sample issue.

VISIT THE JOSSEY-BASS HOME PAGE on the World Wide Web at http://www.josseybass.com for an order form or information about other titles of interest.

National Civic League Publications List

ALL PRICES include shipping and handling (for orders outside the United States, please add $15 for shipping). National Civic League members receive a 10 percent discount. Bulk rates are available. See end of this list for ordering information.

Most Frequently Requested Publications

The Civic Index: A New Approach to Improving Community Life
National Civic League staff, 1993
50 pp., 7 × 10 paper, $7.00

The Community Visioning and Strategic Planning Handbook
National Civic League staff, 1995
53 pp., $23.00

Governance

National Report on Local Campaign Finance Reform
New Politics Program staff, 1998
96 pp., $15.00

Communities and the Voting Rights Act
National Civic League staff, 1996
118 pp., 8.5 × 11 paper, $12.00

Forms of Local Government
National Civic League staff, 1993
15 pp., 5.5 × 8.5 pamphlet, $3.00

Guide for Charter Commissions (Fifth Edition)
National Civic League staff, 1991
46 pp., 6 × 9 paper, $10.00

Handbook for Council Members in Council-Manager Cities (Fifth Edition)
National Civic League staff, 1992
38 pp., 6 × 9 paper, $12.00

Measuring City Hall Performance: Finally, A How-To Guide
Charles K. Bens, 1991
127 pp., 8.5 × 11 monograph, $15.00

Model County Charter (Revised Edition)
National Civic League staff, 1990
53 pp., 5.5 × 8.5 paper, $10.00

Modern Counties: Professional Management—The Non-Charter Route
National Civic League staff, 1993
54 pp., paper, $8.00

Term Limitations for Local Officials: A Citizen's Guide to Constructive Dialogue
Laurie Hirschfeld Zeller, 1992
24 pp., 5.5 × 8.5 pamphlet, $3.00

Using Performance Measurement in Local Government: A Guide to Improving Decisions, Performance, and Accountability
   Paul D. Epstein, 1988
   225 pp., 6 × 9 paper, $5.00

Model City Charter (Seventh Edition)
   National Civic League staff, 1997
   110 pp., 5.5 × 8.5 monograph, $14.00

Alliance for National Renewal

ANR Community Resource Manual
   National Civic League Staff, 1996
   80 pp., 8.5 × 11, $6.00

Taking Action: Building Communities That Strengthen Families
   Special section in *Governing Magazine,* 1998
   8 pp., 8.5 × 11 (color), $3.00

Communities That Strengthen Families
   Insert in *Governing Magazine,* 1997
   8 pp., 8.5 × 11 reprint, $3.00

Connecting Government and Neighborhoods
   Insert in *Governing Magazine,* 1996
   8 pp., 8.5 × 11 reprint, $3.00

The Culture of Renewal
   Richard Louv, 1996
   45 pp., $8.00

The Kitchen Table
   Quarterly newsletter of Alliance for National Renewal, 1999
   8 pp., annual subscription (4 issues) $12.00, free to ANR Partners

The Landscape of Civic Renewal
   Civic renewal projects and studies from around the country, 1999
   185 pp., $12.00

National Renewal
   John W. Gardner, 1995
   27 pp., 7 × 10, $7.00

San Francisco Civic Scan
   Richard Louv, 1996
   100 pp., $6.00

1998 Guide to the Alliance for National Renewal
   National Civic League staff, 1998
   50 pp., 4 × 9, $5.00

Springfield, Missouri: A Nice Community Wrestles with How to Become a Good Community
   Alliance for National Renewal staff, 1996
   13 pp., $7.00

Toward a Paradigm of Community-Making
  Allan Wallis, 1996
  60 pp., $12.00

The We Decade: Rebirth on Community
  Dallas Morning News, 1995
  39 pp., 8.5 × 14 reprint, $3.00

99 Things You Can Do for Your Community in 1999
  poster (folded), $6.00

Healthy Communities

Healthy Communities Handbook
  National Civic League staff, 1993
  162 pp., 8.5 × 11 monograph, $22.00

All-America City Awards

All-America City Yearbook (1991, 1992, 1993, 1994, 1995, 1996, 1997)
  National Civic League staff
  60 pp., 7 × 10 paper, $4.00 shipping and handling

All-America City Awards Audio Tape Briefing
  Audiotape, $4.00 shipping and handling

Diversity and Regionalism

Governance and Diversity:
Findings from Oakland, 1995
Findings from Fresno, 1995
Findings from Los Angeles, 1994
  National Civic League staff
  7 × 10 paper, $5.00 each

Networks, Trust and Values
  Allan D. Wallis, 1994
  51 pp., 7 × 10 paper, $7.00

Inventing Regionalism
  Allan D. Wallis, 1995
  75 pp., 8.5 × 11 monograph, $19.00

Leadership, Collaboration, and Community Building

Citistates: How Urban America Can Prosper in a Competitive World
  Neal Peirce, Curtis Johnson, and John Stuart Hall, 1993
  359 pp., 6.5 × 9.5, $25.00

Collaborative Leadership
  David D. Chrislip and Carl E. Larson, 1994
  192 pp., 6 × 9.5, $20.00

Good City and the Good Life
  Daniel Kemmis, 1995
  226 pp., 6 × 8.5, $23.00

On Leadership
　John W. Gardner, 1990
　220 pp., 6 × 9.5, $28.00

Politics for People: Finding a Responsible Public Voice
　David Mathews, 1994
　229 pp., 6 × 9.5, $20.00

Public Journalism and Public Life
　David "Buzz" Merritt, 1994
　129 pp., 6 × 9, $30.00

Resolving Municipal Disputes
　David Stiebel, 1992
　2 audiotapes and book, $15.00

Time Present, Time Past
　Bill Bradley, former chairman of the National Civic League, 1996
　450 pp., paper, $13.00

Transforming Politics
　David D. Chrislip, 1995
　12 pp., 7 × 10, $3.00

Revolution of the Heart
　Bill Shore, 1996
　167 pp., 8.5 × 5.75, $8.00

The Web of Life
　Richard Louv, 1996
　258 pp., 7.5 × 5.5, $15.00

Programs for Community Problem Solving

Systems Reform and Local Government: Improving Outcomes for Children, Families, and Neighborhoods
　1998, 47 pp., $12.00

Building Community: Exploring the Role of Social Capital and Local Government
　1998, 31 pp., $12.00

The Transformative Power of Governance: Strengthening Community Capacity to Improve Outcomes for Children, Families, and Neighborhoods
　1998, 33 pp., $12.00

Building the Collaborative Community
　Jointly published by the National Civic League and the National Institute for Dispute Resolution, 1994
　33 pp., $12.00

Negotiated Approaches to Environmental Decision Making in Communities: An Exploration of Lessons Learned
　Jointly published by the National Institute for Dispute Resolution and the Coalition to Improve Management in State and Local Government, 1996
　58 pp., $14.00

Community Problem Solving Case Summaries, Volume III
  1992, 52 pp., $19.00

Facing Racial and Cultural Conflicts: Tools for Rebuilding Community (Second Edition)
  1994, $24.00

Collaborative Transportation Planning Guidelines for Implementing ISTEA and the CAAA
  1993, 87 pp., $14.00

Collaborative Planning Video
  Produced by the American Planning Association, 1995
  6-hr. video and 46 pp. workshop materials, $103.00

Pulling Together: A Land Use and Development Consensus Building Manual
  A joint publication of PCPS and the Urban Land Institute, 1994
  145 pp., $34.00

Solving Community Problems by Consensus
  1990, 20 pp., $14.00

Involving Citizens in Community Decision Making: A Guidebook
  1992, 30 pp., $30.00

NATIONAL CIVIC LEAGUE sales policies: Orders must be paid in advance by check, VISA, or MasterCard. We are unable to process exchanges, returns, credits, or refunds. For orders outside the United States, add $15 for shipping.

TO PLACE AN ORDER:

CALL the National Civic League at (303) 571–4343 or (800) 223–6004, or

MAIL ORDERS TO:
  National Civic League
  1445 Market Street, Suite 300
  Denver, CO 80202–1717, or

E-MAIL the National Civic League at ncl@ncl.org